1

BOYS

LIKE

ME

James Colwell

Preface

<u>Why Now?</u>

The one question that sets itself firmly in my mind as to the premise of this book is very simple. Why now? Why is now the time to write this book, what have you done and what truth have you discovered that qualifies you to write this information now?

Repair is my answer. I need to fix what is broken within me and in the process sharing the **FACTS** about my life, I hope will bless someone to repair their life as well or completely deter them from making the mistakes I have made. There is someone out there that needs to hear my version of life – everyone has a story, it's true, I feel as though mine needs to be shared. There is a little boy out

there who has too much twitch in his walk and not enough
bass in his voice who is waiting to hear, that it is okay.
There is a little boy out there that has a family that pretends
to be okay with the sexuality that belongs to him. There is
a mother out there that is willing to stand her ground in her
beliefs and do it without having to throw her child away.
There are family members that are not willing to stand in
their truth about the part they have played in creating a
hostile environment for this little boy who has always had
way too much swag. There are people from all walks of
life that do not have a clear picture of what it is to be
homosexual and what it entails on a day-to-day basis. And
there is **ME**, a normal everyday person who has dealt with
all of these situations and does not claim to have all the
answers but is willing to share the good and bad, the ups
and downs, the totally hurtful and the undeniably
empowering times of my life with all the honesty and
transparency that I can stand! Now is the time to do this
because I am at the opposite side of my issues and I am

repairing myself daily and I want to help others who have

or happen to be a **BOY LIKE ME!**

ONE

<u>Life - Love - Jokes</u>

Winter seems to always bring surprises, you can never tell what the weather is going to be – clear skies or snow up to your knees. This theme even carried over to the maternity ward on January 9, 1972, a single mother gave birth to a baby boy that she lovingly named James Edwin Colwell. This same child was given a nickname of "**Shaft**," that came directly from a movie that would become a cult classic that told the story of a private detective that was suave, street smart, and irresistible to women. Well that is where the joke went into play – in what seemed, no time at all it would become extremely evident that this little boy was the furthest thing from that character that you could even imagine. He had an overabundance of swag and charisma, but he lacked in masculinity totally. Just as docile as could be was this little creature, he was as full of life as anything and anyone could hope for. Surrounded constantly by his immediate family he thrived, in many ways. No cares in the world for three and a half years and then his mother came home with an addition, a very small boy; a brother.

James learned right away that life isn't always going to be fair and it doesn't always go as planned. He had been told that his mother was having a baby, but it was more than that; he understood that she was having two babies, called a set of twins. But for some reason she returned with only one. It was confusing and seemed so unfair. Right there is where the whole feeling of being slighted or just simply not getting all that was inevitably yours took its root in the little boy. As he matured he would deal constantly with not accepting less than what he was due. And most of this would be in the form of relationships. One of the strongest, non-changing relationships was formed the day that baby came home; although he didn't really know exactly how to feel about this new member of his household, he basically went along with the program and it was like clockwork, in a very short time he grew to love that baby and would from there and forever protect that baby from everything but his own wrath. In the early days it became evident that the two of them were like night and day. He was neat and kept things in an orderly fashion; that baby was a slob and seemed to like to live in clutter. He was obedient and stayed out of his mother's way; that baby has never been big on listening and has been challenging his mama this whole journey. The two of them don't really see eye to eye for the most part and that baby seems to always get his way; it was really no big deal, that's just the way it is. Spoiled rotten, that's what he was and still is to this day. Spoiled by his mother and his older brother. He was a preemie with a still-born twin; that's how he entered the world. That's a heavy load, so his family has always allowed for a little space for him. Why not, he is the baby.

The mother of these two boys is a very up front, outspoken individual who, from what I can see, has always had her two children at the beginning and the end of every decision she has made since she had them. Very strong willed in her approach and vision for the eldest of the two boys she was and still is. And as always, there is still that little bit of space that has been given to that youngest child.

Though I love my mother with every fiber that I am made up of, I have always felt that there was a slight bit of bullying that has always been evident when it involves me. It started early on in our lives, but the reality is, she has always realized that one child would listen and the other one was a bit defiant. And I believe she picked her battles, up to the age of 18 my mother more or less pushed me around in areas that she knew not to even approach with my brother, because she was going to lose, hands down. I have to say, I don't believe that baby has ever completed a punishment period. I think he got put on punishment and was told that he would not be allowed out to play once when he was about 6 and just literally never got off of that punishment. Reason being, when we would go to my grandmothers' house for her to babysit us, any punishment I was on was being enforced totally, no matter what. Rather it be no television (I have always been a lover of the boob-tube), no outside or whatever it was, my grandmother was behind it 200%. One time in particular, my mom had forgot to tell my grandmother that I had been removed from a punishment that I was on, I was made miserable all day long because she wouldn't take my word for it and I was held to the confinements of that punishment until she spoke with my mother. I found it to be cruel, especially when I was not a child that told lies. My brother on the other hand, was handled in a totally different manner. Ten minutes after my mom left, so did he. The only punishment that ever worked on him was, not being allowed to go outdoors. But it really didn't work because he didn't stay inside. He would tell my grandmother, "What is she gonna do, kill me! She will put me back on punishment." And out the door he would go. I tease my Mom all the time now; I tell her, "You were horrible at issuing punishment to your baby; you would go out the front door and he would go out the back door." We have shared many laughs about that situation over the years. But the difference in the way we were handled was extremely evident when it came to schooling. When I graduated from high school I was 17 and my plan was to attend school for fashion design. Well, this was so far from what my mother had in mind. And that is where an old argument resurfaced. There was a woman that was a neighbor of ours when I was growing up named

Vivian Younger, who was a good friend of my mom's. She recognized my creativity and thirst to learn way back when I was about 6 or 7, and she taught me to crochet, knit, macramé and various styles of beadwork. Miss Vivian could also sew, she is one of the most talented, self-taught individuals that I have ever met, and I am forever grateful to her for turning my creative light on. She used to talk to me about sewing, she didn't feel as strongly about her sewing abilities as she did about her beadwork and manipulation of threads. She would always explain to me about the limitations of not knowing how to draft patterns; she always told me that I would have to learn pattern-making because I was too talented to have any limits. I never forgot that, and before I leave the planet I have all intentions on teaching her everything I know about pattern-making. I thought that goal would never happen, when she moved away and we lost contact years ago, but she has moved back recently and I will be able to give my mentor the gift I feel she is so deserving. She always speaks so highly of my talent and I don't know if she really knows that I have always been in awe of the things that she can do. She has the hands of an angel and those hands do some amazing things. Miss Viv and my Mom would always have ongoing dialog about what I was going to do when I grew up. My mom was dead-set that I was going to be a computer programmer with a business degree and she definitely put in the funds to make this a reality. I was learning programming by the time I was in third grade and I was supplied with a lot of things that many children my age didn't have. When everyone was playing Intellivison and Atari, I was spending time learning to manipulate figures and program lingo on my Radio Shack TRS-80 Color Computer. I was not denied the video games, we had them too, but the computer was my mother's preferred form of entertainment. The more I learned the more she invested, buying printers and scanners and whatever else I requested. While Miss Vivian stood steady in telling my mother, "I hate to hurt your feelings, but he is going to be doing something with his hands." They would never agree on this subject. Ultimately, Miss Vivian would be victorious in that argument. But to my knowledge, I don't think she ever told my mom, "I told you so."

The road to my decision of what to do with myself was grueling with the constant argument between my mother and I. Upon my graduation from Langley High School, I was forced to apply and attend Community College Allegheny Campus with a full-time class schedule and a major of Business Management. I continued with this charade for one full year before I found myself so miserable that I had to do something. My grades began to drop along with my attendance record; I got so discouraged with my situation that I couldn't even stand to listen to what the instructors were talking about. I hated the sight of the buildings, even when I just drove past the campus I felt an uneasiness in my stomach. I kept up appearances for my family, I literally got up everyday and went to school, but I never got out of my car. I sat in my vehicle for hours each day sketching clothing designs and dreaming of chasing my passion for the creative. When my class hours were over I would go home and sew for the rest of the day. It was a miserable existence, living a lie has never been my type of life. By this time I had turned 18 and was getting a bit fed up, I always knew that this situation was strange and I knew no one else who was enduring this, but I had never defied my mother. My brother did it all the time, so how bad could it be, I figured she'll be mad but it won't last and she will understand. One day as I was sitting in my car I decided to drive into downtown Pittsburgh and visit The Clarissa School of Fashion Design. I was welcomed and taken on a tour of the school and equipped with an application filled with questions about my interest in fashion and my skill level. I sat there and completed the forms, took a deep breath and turned it in, two weeks later I got an acceptance letter. I then figured, it was time to come clean because there was no option; I was going to attend. So I left my bedroom and took my letter downstairs to the kitchen where I found my grandmother and a close family friend that I have always called my aunt, they were having lunch like they did everyday. I explained to them what had be going on and what my intentions were, after being shocked, they both agreed that I should be going to school

for whatever subject I choose. My Grandmother said in her

normal colorful way of expression, "You're the one that's

gotta do it, tell your mother, 'To hell with her.' Let her

take her ass to business school and get a business degree."

We laughed, as we always did, my grandmother has never

had a filter on her mouth, anything may come out of there

at anytime.

Well now the edge had been taken off, with my grandma

backing me, what's the worst that could happen? So I let

my Gram know that I would tell my mom when she came

from work. I was living with my Grandmother at this time,

but my Mother came by everyday for dinner when she got

off work. When I heard my mom come through the door I

got up from the sewing machine and came down to talk to

her. My Grandma promptly came into the diningroom and

took a seat at the table as I explained to my mother my

dilemma and what my plans were. I watched as her face

hardened like one of the witches from a Walt Disney

animated movie, and then she began, "You are the dumbest

ass I have ever met; you are not dropping out of CCAC to go to some dead end sewing school. Go there for what, you already know how to sew, what in the shit are they suppose to teach you. You are going to get my business degree and get a job, that sewing shit ain't gonna get you a job. You will not sit around here being a starving artist, that's bullshit!" She stood up from the table and began making herself a plate from the stove, my Grandmother looked at me as if to say, 'Okay, now what's next.' I told my mother, I didn't agree and I was already withdrawn from CCAC. Well that did it, it got very loud from that point on, but really to me it all sound like the teachers on Charlie Brown (whomp-whomp-whomp-whomp). Then she said something that caught my ear and infuriated me; she yelled, "So since you think you're grown, that's how you're gonna be, don't ask me for a damn thing, you take care of yourself, because that's what grown folks do!" And then out of left field, the unthinkable happened. My Grandmother chimed in with, "I agree, when you are too grown to listen to your Mother, you are on your own!" I was thinking, 'Really, I had no plans on asking you for anything anyway. But are you serious, when did my Grandma become a complete turn-coat?' The way she was carrying on, I didn't even want anything coming from that direction anyway. I had become very evil and upset – this just happens to be part of my personality, I started my life a little docile but that didn't last very long. Although I love my Mother with every piece of my being, I won't accept bad behavior from her, and this was classified in my files as BAD BEHAVIOR. She was being ridiculously unreasonable; she was not open to listen to reasoning or anything, all she was focused on what her vision for my life was, which I have to say was so far off of the mark. Ultimately her reason for acting this way was a form of bullying, and a reaction to the fear of losing the control that she possessed and used for so long over this child that for years she knew was **different**. I believe that my mother feels that she can protect me better if she chooses, controls and guides my steps, and that is where her comfort zone is, still to this day. For that reason, I was able to live through this 'schooling fiasco' and come out on the other side with my self-worth at an all time high; a degree in Apparel Technology and my mother sitting up front at my graduation. I also did something that was not very easy for me to do, and still isn't – I FORGAVE. I forgave my mother for what I felt was poor treatment, it had nothing to do with monetary things, all the highs and lows that go along with obtaining a degree were left with me and me alone, I had no cheering section at home, just nay-sayers. I made my way through those two years of school without asking for or accepting anything from anyone in my family other than poor treatment. The treatment was poor because you never heard the end of it, my mother just could not let it go, and she made me know constantly that she felt the wrong decision was made, she babbled on about it all the way up to my graduation. And then she began her babble again one month later – when she realized I had enrolled in The Pittsburgh Beauty Academy for Cosmetology. Yes, the sparks flew and the argument about my future was again at an all time high.

25

TWO

<u>The Center Of My Joy,</u>

<u>Uh – Not So Much</u>

Everybody has one family member that they are just linked to the hip with, and it is so funny how time will repeat itself. The person that I was the most attached to was my Grandmother, her name is Thelma Colwell. And I see the exact same thing with my Mother and my youngest son; trying to separate him from my mother is next to impossible, it's like trying to separate two ice cubes. And I understand because as I was growing up my Grandmother couldn't get a break, I wanted to be everywhere she was.

It was such a funny dynamic to have, I remember having to always explain to people that there was nothing going on between my Mom and I, or at her home. I just preferred spending time with my Grandma. I loved my Thelma, she wasn't perfect and I knew that from a very young age but that didn't matter she was my center and she always made me feel wanted and safe. She is a short, thick built dark-skinned woman with the most beautiful skin; I always wanted to be as dark as her because she had no blemishes and told me she had never had one. I didn't either but I could see what lighter-skinned African Americans went through. My Mother is dark-skinned just like my Grandma and I, but my Aunt(my mother's sister) is a lighter-skinned woman with naturally red hair and grey eyes and she has always had battles with her skin. I've always embraced my dark skin. Thelma has always had a gorgeous head of long thick hair, I have distinct memories of the smells that permeated the area when my Grandma would wash and condition her hair. Should used that cheap Suave shampoo and conditioner she would get from the grocery store, then she would buy an expensive little glass tube of Infusium 23. I'd watch as she'd break the tip and say, "Back up, this is good shit right here!" Then she would blow dry her hair, add a little bit of Liv hair crème, and blow dry til it was completely dry and either put pink sponge rollers in it or if she were going somewhere right then she would use her curling iron. I watched her do this regime so many hundreds of times that it is not surprising that I became a licensed cosmetologist. I eventually moved into the house with my Grandmother and Great-Grandmother when I grew ultimately tired of the constant interaction with my Aunt's two sons. They spent a lot of time at my Mom's house, and so did their friends and a few other cousins, hanging along side of them. The ridicule was too much and it got to a point where I was finding myself wanting to seriously hurt them. Then my Aunt's oldest son got shot and ended up being confined to a wheelchair and moved in with my Mom for awhile due to the layout of her apartment. At that point, it was a wrap, I was out of there, I never even considered living with my Mom again.

My Grandmother's house was like a train station at times, there was always someone having to stay with us. They were either trying to transition to something or somewhere, or estranged from a mate. A bit of a flop house if you will. But naturally my family would try to color it up as, 'Oh, it's the family house,' or 'Aunt Thelma helps everyone.' Actually what it was in my eyes was an overactive dumping ground for those losing at life in most cases. My Grandmother was sitting on a sly movement of collecting whatever monies that she could from whoever she could, with the pretense of being the helpful Aunt or old time friend. The funny thing was, as slick as she thought she was, she was always on the losing end of these arrangements. I remember counting the number of keys that were out in the atmosphere at one time, and there were eighteen people who had active working keys to our house, that is RIDICULOUS. But even with all that, all I needed to be comfortable was knowing that my Grandmother was there and I was going to be there with her.

Being around my Grandmother was a never-ending journey into funny sayings and curse words. My Gram was known throughout the family for her lack of tact and use of foul language; she could curse most folks under the table. And she would say things that sometimes took years for me to figure out, but were so funny that you couldn't wait to hear it again. She is someone that I definitely believe has missed their calling to be a comedian. She's ridiculous, and I have always found it to be a riot. I was always listening even when she thought I wasn't; I heard it all, from the family goings on, to the advice and reactions to advice not taken by the girls in the family. One time my Aunt came to the house and asked my Gram to borrow money to go to bingo and my Gram blurted out, "Huh, I'm not giving you shit; if you sell that pussy instead of giving it away, you'd have enough money to go anywhere you wanted go." I just hung my head over the bed and acted like I was still watching television, but my insides were shaking from laughter, I was about 7 years old at the time. Oh my she had such sayings. Some things I heard so often that I automatically put them to memory, and have found myself living by them – and most of them were meant for the female members of the family (and me indirectly). A few of Miss Colwell's anecdotes were…

I'm no free fucking whore!

(one of her favorites)

You crackin' but you fackin'

(meaning - your joking but, you don't even realize it's true)

Don't let Julia fool ya

(for the longest time I couldn't figure out 'Who the hell

Julia was')

I'll knock your dick outdoors

(well...)

Who knew that my lessons of Curse 101 would come in handy, and trust me it did almost immediately, I have a way of expressing myself that isn't always the nicest when I see fit. It's like being bilingual, but you really can't use the skill in the workplace.

I was not really permitted to use that language, but I took it everywhere with me and used it as I saw fit, and still do. I definitely know how to get your attention and let you know what I think blatantly. I have no problem being as offensive as it takes to back you up into your lane, and keep you there. Where my Mom would get upset about the things that came out of my mouth, my Grandmother would sometimes finish what parts I left off. One time that sticks

out in my mind is when my Uncle and I got into it. My

Uncle was just that, the only uncle I had and my

Grandmother's only son. He drank a lot and lived at

another, what I would call, flop house up the street from us.

The only difference was the people who lived there didn't

pretend they were living in any different environment, they

owned it. The house wreaked of stale liquor and so did it's

inhabitants. On this particular day, my Uncle's daughter

was visiting with me at my Grandma's house and she

decided to go up and ask her dad for money, so we went

together like we did everything else when we were

together, she was my absolute favorite cousin while

growing up. We protected each other and did things the

way cousins are supposed to. We had such totally different

raisings and rules we had to abide by, but it never entered

our world, we loved each other and that was that. I

absolutely adored my Uncle as well, when I was younger

he would periodically take me out early in the day with his

friends, we went downtown to a place called Big Z's that

had the best breakfast you've ever tasted and they served booze. My uncle and his friends would talk stuff for hours; my Uncle was the only one that could come close to out cursing my Grandma. Hanging out with my Uncle was a great time, but not really age appropriate for an 8 year old. My Mom would've died if she knew, but my Grandma would let me go. One of my fondest memories is when my Uncle and his friends took me to the movie theatre to see Purple Rain the movie. It was great and I've never forgot that day with my Uncle Georgie. But overshadowing that memory is the memory of standing in the hallway at age 11 while my cousin went into the livingroom of my uncle's place and listening as he came from out of nowhere and told my first cousin, "I don't want you spending as much time with Shaft, he's a bad influence." I couldn't believe what I was hearing, my cousin automatically became combative with her dad. I then entered the room and watched as my uncle's face was like a deer caught in headlights, I stood in front of him and said, "And just what the hell about me is a bad influence on her?" All he would say is, "You know!" I helped him out and told him, "No I don't know what you are talking about but I will tell you this…" and I preceded to curse my Uncle out thoroughly. In the midst of it, the woman who's house my Uncle lived in, tried to intervene by saying she thought the way I was talking to him was wrong, so I cursed her out too. She called my Grandmother and told her what was going on. She then told me my Grandmother sent word for me to come home immediately. My cousin and I left after I was done telling them just what I thought of them and their living arrangements. I made sure I let my Uncle know that I would never speak to him ever again as long as I lived. (A promise that I absolutely kept.) Once my cousin got back down to my Grandmother's place I was seething with anger, my Grandmother wanted an explanation and no sooner than I told her what happened, my Gram snatched the phone and called my Uncle and cursed him out and asked to speak to the female friend and cursed her out and told her not to ever call her with a half of a story ever again and told her to mind her business next time. My Uncle died a few years after this situation took place and it has always been a sad episode to me; it felt unfinished, because I could not say to my Uncle exactly what I wanted and felt, because I didn't want to hurt my cousins' feelings. He was going on and on about me being a bad influence on her and that was so far from the truth. We are a year and nine days apart, and at the time this took place my cousin was 12; she was already having sex with multiple partners, drinking beer and smoking marijuana. I wasn't indulging in any of these things and still don't. And the most hilarious part to this is how life plays out, my Uncle's precious daughter turned out to be a crackhead and I have adopted two of her children. So he got his wish; none of my so-called unsavory ways rubbed off on her.(I know complete sarcasm, I'm working on that!)

I started to realize a difference in my feelings toward my Grandmother and some of her decisions as I reached my teenage years, and it really had a lot to do with her love of money. The woman who once fought relentlessly to make certain nobody bothered me, had turned into this little money grubbing midget in my eyes. Everything was about rent payment and how you had better have your rent in. And it wasn't across the board, some folks were just plain ole' getting over. I was aggravated by my little leprechaun at least twenty days out of the month about money that she received every month on the same day, it was crazy. My Mother had always given my Grandmother money to accommodate my stay with her and by the time I turned 10 years old my Mother had a court ordered child support check that came every month, unbeknownst to everyone, my Mother has never cashed one of these checks, she has always forwarded them directly to my Grandmother for the care of me, and when the child support order was done I paid out of my own pocket. She has never received a payment late or short, yet fussed about how she'd better get it all month long. She would even go so far as to lead people to believe that I was living off of her.

One day my cousin (my Grandmother's sister's eldest daughter) called to our house to speak to me, she asked if I would come over to her house so we can sit down and talk,

I replied, "Of course." Once I was there, she sat me down and went through this whole scenario about how bad my Grandmother's finances were and the fact that I had a part time job after school and how it isn't right that I don't contribute anything to the household. Well, of course I became upset and explained about the monies that my Grandmother had been receiving, while my cousin sat there like a deer caught in headlights. I nicely explained that the next time she want to play the finance game with me she would need to have all her facts straight. She felt like I was getting smart, it wasn't my intent but in essence I guess I was; but no apology was owed, she was being nebby and was completely out of order, I thought, to be approaching the subject.

So many times my Grandmother sat back and played the victim while throwing rocks and hiding her hands. The worst time of all was when I was in cosmetology school; it was the day after Christmas, I came in from attending school and an evening haircutting tutorial and as I approached my bedroom I knew immediately, something wasn't right. Well as it turned out, my so called favorite

cousin had come in earlier that day and stolen my video

camera, two pair of gold earring, one pair of silver earring

and my brand new diamond earrings that I received just the

day before. I was very upset, to which my grandmother

replied, "Well hell, it is not my job to sit here and watch

your shit while you run the streets." That was an idiotic

statement and I let her know it. My Grandmother filed

charges against my cousin (which didn't stick because she

testified in court that she didn't see the items in her hands

physically) and filed a claim against her home owner's

insurance. Well it took months for this check to come, so I

thought. I happened to be in my Grandmother's room

looking for something and I came across the paystub from

the check issued by the insurance company. When I

approached my Grandmother she started to rant and rave

about how I didn't ever pay an insurance premium and the

money was rightfully hers and she wasn't going to give me

all that money to mess up. After an extensive shouting

match and a threat to contact the insurance company an

claim insurance fraud, she decided to give me what was left of my check. The original check was for over $700, she gave me less than $250. I basically got robbed twice.

Even after that situation she kept trying to raise my rent to $300 once the child support order was over and the rent was being paid out of my pocket. I explained to her that the mortgage payment on the house was only $270 and there was no way I was going to pay that kind of money and live in her house and her scrutiny. It was a very aggravating process, it was like paying your rent on time and receiving an eviction notice everyday for the last twenty days of the month. It made no sense. I eventually grew tired of the deceptive happenings and foolishness and left home at 22.

It was in my eyes a sad turn of events; the woman that I once couldn't get enough of being around, I all of a sudden couldn't get away from fast enough!

THREE

Everybody Isn't Picking On You

I can admit that I have several pet peeves that I have never been able to shake, but the worst one of all is when I hear an adult say to a child, "Everyone isn't picking on you!"

During the earlier years of my life I found out fairly quickly that there was no truth to this statement. By the age of 8, I was experiencing days when actually everyone was picking on me and it caused me to internalize a lot of the pain which played a large part in me become an angry child. When you are receiving criticism and bullying from all angles, who do you turn to for help or even just to discuss the situation? I experienced verbal abuse from adults and teenagers in my family and whenever I was outside playing or in school there was abuse coming from the children in my age group as well. I use to rattle my brain trying to figure out how everyone around me got onto the same page about what they felt was wrong with me, and how that conclusion was decided upon. After becoming an adult I realized, that the children in my age group took on the bad behavior of the teens and adults that they witnessed dishing out the abuse, I have a hard time believing such young children even knew the meaning of some of the things that were being said to me. A lot of the time people would say demeaning things to me and I had no idea what they were talking about, but I could tell by the way it was said, that it was meant to be insulting. The truth is, some of the things that were thrown out at me, didn't make any sense to me until I was about 18 or 19 years old. A lot of comments were very physical in nature and I wasn't a sexually charged preteen, so much of it went over my head. Though I was around older people and more mature conversations the connection wasn't there for me to make. No one in my surroundings was having open talks about gay life or homosexual sex acts; these topics only arose when someone was trying to offend or degrade me.

The first memory of an insult that I endured and had no idea of the origin was when I was just 6 years old. I remember like it was yesterday, the venom of what was being said and the stabbing action that it took against my being. It was the first time I had ever heard the word **FAGGOT**. I had no idea what that was or what it referred to, but immediately when it was said, I knew that it wasn't anything good. The person spewing the venom, was my Great-Grandmother, her name was Sally Mary Wesley and she was a very two sided woman with a face to match, she had a pure Church Mothers face for the public and a dark soulless mug for inside the house. She lived in the house with my Grandmother, and it was evident to me early on that I wasn't one of her favorite people. Shortly afterwards I started letting her know that the feelings were mutual. On this particular day, six year old me was doing what I always did, spending time in my own world, I entertained myself a lot through music and art, they were the two things I loved most. I was dancing and singing as I went into the kitchen for a glass of water, and out of nowhere, Sally Mae reared her head of salt and pepper hair and said, "Sit down

somewhere, ya' lil' faggot!" When I turned and made eye

contact with her there was a look of disgust on her face that

would remain whenever she had to deal with me until she

laid down and died in the Winter of 1997. I never bothered

telling anyone about what was said, what was the point I

thought; she was my Grandmother's Mother and my

Mother's grandmother – what could they do? A little while

after that I found out exactly what could be done, her bad

behavior continued to the point that it became evident to

my Mother that differences were being made between me

and my brother when it came to Momma Sal, as most of the

grandchildren called her; the great-grandchildren called

her, Gram and we all called my Grandmother by her first

name. There were many times that I would witness Gram

giving my brother money to go to the store or giving him

candy and treats and she act just like I didn't exist. I never

let that bother me, because there were two truths that

couldn't be changed and they were – I loved my brother

and I didn't like her. My Mother started to take notice and

take action, there were times when she would sneak and do her distribution and if my Mom was around, she would make my Brother give the candy or the money back to her, then would tell her, "If you don't give both, you don't give either!" Gram learned to just do it when my Mom wasn't around, truly I didn't care. The big fall out came one Christmas when I was 9; when my Mom, my Brother and I got to my Grandma's house for the family holiday dinner and all of my immediate family was there. We were actually the last ones to get there. We were all at the tables eating when my mother opened the individual envelopes that Mama Sal had given her for my Brother and I (which she did every year). My mother handed both envelopes back to her with all the contents intact and then stated to her, "I told you before, I will never allow you to make a difference between my children. If you can't give them the same or treat them the same, they don't need anything from you, period." Gram was very shady in her way of thinking and doing things, she didn't argue, she didn't fuss, she just accepted her gift back and was very unapologetic in doing so. My Mother made reference to how she had been doing this stuff throughout the years to other members of the family. Everybody was quiet like they didn't know what she was talking about, but my mom just politely pointed out who the abused persons were. My Great-Grandmother never apologized or denied the accusations.

Now I can't say that I understand liking one of your children or grandchildren better than the other, but I know it does happen; but the part that puzzles me is when you pick and choose and then blatantly mistreat the one that isn't your pick. It was a horrible family dynamic and it started way before I ever became a part of this dysfunctional unit.

Over the years I have pieced together what had really been happening before we got to the mistreatment of this **different** little boy. It went like this…

Sally Mary Wesley (my Great-Grandmother) had two daughters…

Thelma (my Grandmother) (*Sally mistreated*)

Louise (*Sally's pick*)

Thelma had three children...

Girl #1 (my Aunt) (*Sally's pick*)

Boy (my Uncle)

Girl #2 (my Mother)

Louise had five children...

Boy #1 (*Sally's pick*)

Girl #1

Girl #2 (*Sally mistreated*)

Boy #2

Boy #3

My Aunt had two children...

Boy #1 (*Sally's pick*)

Boy #2

My Uncle had two children...

Boy

Girl

My Mom had two children…

Boy #1 (me) *(Sally mistreated)*

Boy #2 *(Sally's pick)*

If you were not one of Sally's picks or mistreated, you were basically ignored like you didn't really exist. I did notice that my Grandmother's sisters' children didn't come around Gram very much once they were old enough to make their own decisions. She lived in the house with my Grandmother, so unfortunately, we were subject to her scrutiny and hateful behavior full time.

She gave dirty looks and things most of the time and just kind of ignored you the rest of the time, but after awhile that was not effective on me; by the time I was ten or eleven I had a strong dislike for her, so I really took her lead and acted like she wasn't there most of the time. I had reduced her to hello and goodbye. But she and I would butt heads once more when I was thirteen years old, this particular day my cousin and I got into a verbal battle, he is my Aunt's eldest child and happens to be ten years older than I am and a paraplegic. I don't even remember how it started or what it was about but I know the basis was what it always was, showing off. He had two of our other cousins with him and he was really doing it up for them. I was in the livingroom, while the three of them and Mama Sal were in the kitchen. My first cousin spewed sissy and faggot like they were the words of the month. Then he went into a whole regime of, "You're gonna be just like Plotka when you grow up. (I had no idea what a Plotka was. – I found out years later that Plotka was a drag queen from our neighborhood that was our parents' age.) He went on and on as the laughter in the kitchen reached its peak, it was like I was at a comedy show and I was the butt of every joke. After about 20 minutes the name calling and slurs had escalated to a level that I wasn't willing to continue with. I then came to life in a mighty way and began to insult him back, my Great-Grandmother, who had been as quiet as a church mouse, blurted out, "You'd better watch your mouth boy!" I stood up and went into the kitchen and approached her and said, "Are you serious, you just sat here for the last half hour and listened to him call me everything but a child of God and now you are chastising me for defending myself." She just look at me with that dismissive shady look and said, "Go somewhere and sit down, now!" At that point, the gloves were off and I thoroughly cursed him out with no filter being used, I was pretty harsh I must say, ending my rant referring to him as 'iron side.' The comment shut him down and made her rise to her feet and approach me, she and I stood face to face as I asked her, "What are you going to do about it, because you know my Mother will handle you if you put your hands on me." She deflated and told me I had better go sit down, to which I replied, "When I'm ready!"

I'm not proud of the outcome of the sorted dynamic between my Great-Grandmother and I. Even back then I thought it was sad, most people don't ever get to meet their great-grandparents and here I am constantly battling and arguing with mine, just ridiculous.

After that day, I reduced my dealing with her to a non-existence, I literally said nothing to her, ever. I didn't even feel as though she was worth the words.

Not long after this, my Grandmother's sister past away, it was awful. My Grandmother was devastated, her and her sister were closer than any two people I ever knew, they literally talked on the phone every morning at about 5 a.m. It was like clockwork, but all that had come to an end. This was the first time in my life that someone so closely related has died and my family was forced to deal with it. At this place is a terrible memory embedded into my psyche, and it isn't the death or the funeral that followed. The memory is of the moment I realized how treacherous, shameless and brutally honest my Great Grandmother could be. The situation took place the day after my Grandmother's sister passed away, we were standing in the hallway on the second floor of our home, my Grandmother and I were on our way downstairs to have some lunch when the unexplainable happened. As we passed my Great Grandmother in the hallway, out of nowhere she said to my

Grandmother, "It should've been you that died and not my Louise!" I thought I was in the Twilight Zone. I couldn't believe the nerve of her to say that; who even thinks that way. I watched as my Grandmother's face just dropped and it was the first time that I've ever seen my Grandmother cry. And it broke my heart, I couldn't believe what I was seeing happen. My Great Grandmother never flinched, she just kept walking down the hallway and went into her room. As I followed my Grandmother down the stairs I said to her, "Surely, she needs to move out of here. How can she say that to you in your own house. What kind of mother says that?" She responded, "Hush up boy, it's fine, everything is going to be fine, sit your grown behind down."

I left that situation alone for the time, but I never forgave Sally Mary Wesley for her indiscretions, she died in December of 1997 and I have tried to let go of the ill feelings I have toward my Great Grandmother, to no avail. I never wanted to understand why she was the way she was, all I know is I never want to be like her!

There was also another person in my immediate family who was relentless in their pursuit to make sure that I was miserable growing up. The strange thing about that person is he was my Mother's absolute favorite person. He was my Aunt's youngest son, before I was born my Mother spent a lot of time with him, he was like her baby, she actually gave me his first name as my middle name. And as far back as I can remember, I hated it and him. My family always had this strange way of trying to mask one thing and call it another. The dysfunction of myself and my first cousin's relationship for years was blamed on a lie, and that is what it was, a lie that I was jealous of the relationship between my cousin and my Mother. The truth is I had no interest in being around my Mother, because we had nothing in common. When I was a young child, I never related to my Mother as anything more than my creator until I was in my mid-twenties. That is when our relationship was built, I stuck up under my Grandmother from a young child and that's where I stayed until adulthood. This particular cousin as I said was relentless, I

have wracked my brain in this process to try to remember a
positive moment with this person during my early days and
I come up with nothing. I don't ever recall anything but
insults coming from him, and when there was ever a crowd
around things got worse. The only time when he backed
off was if my Mother was present. You name it, he called
me it – faggot, sissy, bitch – you name it. Other family
members who were of age to stop the torment basically
witnessed it and laughed along with the crowd or acted as if
they didn't notice it. The older I got the worse the situation
got, the insults became more intense, verbally it was
nothing less than vicious. By the age of 11 or 12, I had
began to stand up for myself and I was as verbally out of
order as he was, I would curse him completely out. And at
the point, a nasty little game started to be played. By the
time I reached my pre teen years I was getting tired of
being a punching bag for anyone and I had begun to fight
back, I experienced anger in the worst way, a lot of times I
would lose control. So what would happen was the loss of
control would be the thing that was being focused on and

not the origin of what caused the bad behavior. When

episodes would take place my Mother would be made

aware of the episodes by my first cousin and older cousins

and led her to believe that I just flew off the handle

basically for no reason, and I began to be punished for

these outbreaks. My Mother's main issue and why I would

be being punished most times had to do with the fact that

my Grandmother would be upset, and my Mom's favorite

line was, "You are not going to give my mother a heart

attack with your bullshit!" I would get punishment in the

form of staying in the house or having to go stay down at

her house for a period of time. The fact of the matter is that

my Grandmother swept too much bad behavior under the

rug and my Mother just flat out didn't pay enough

attention. I was content staying with my Grandma and my

Mother figured that everything was fine, but that is no

excuse, she dropped the ball. She was not in touch with

what was actually going on with me like she should have,

she left too much trust in her Mother, and my Grandmother

was playing the, 'It's all going good game.'

The biggest blowup with my antagonizing cousin happened after he had moved away, got married, came back alone on the brink of a divorce, more immature and more self-centered than he was originally. He was at an all time high of ridiculous behavior and on this particular day he went way too far with me and so did the rest of the family that were present. My Grandmother was throwing a birthday celebration for her very good friend that day, it was July 29th, so the heat was at it peak, which was never a good time for me (I really don't like hot weather that much, I don't know how we made it back then without central air units!) I awoke and everything seemed to be going well until I decided to go down to the basement for something and there was my cousin sprawled out sleep on one of the beds that was down there. The other was being used by an older cousin that I would refer to as an uncle (due to the age difference) who would stay with us too often when he and his wife were on the outs. Within minutes I was literally pissed off at the sight of my first cousin, he was wearing a brand new outfit that belonged to me, that was in a drawer in that basement with the tags on it when I went to sleep the night before. I woke him up and told him to take my clothes off, to which the name calling started. But it wasn't going to go that smoothly, I wasn't receptive to his mouthing off on that day and I tried to avoid the normal scene by going and telling my Grandmother what was happening. She basically blew me off, which caused me to yell at her. By this time my cousin had gotten out of the bed and came to the first floor and so did my older cousin, both were a little pissed about being woke up, but who cares. At that point I was 15 and paying rent monthly and neither one of them were, so really who cares. My cousin had become so comfortable with his disrespect of me that he just went ahead and labeled me all kinds of gay insults just like my Grandmother wasn't present in that kitchen, but she might as well not have been, because she didn't say a word until I began to curse him out, and call him all types of washed up losers. And of course with me always being around adults, I had the 411 on his situation so when I spoke, I spoke of truth and I cut deep and cut fast (by this time the sharpness of my tongue had taken it's place in the World,

thoroughly). Well as usual I was on my own to defend

myself, so I let the fur fly. My Grandmother sent me to my

room, which was on the second floor across the hall from

the bathroom. Within minutes my cousin was upstairs in

the bathroom slinging insults across the hall. It was

pointless, it was just as though the mistreatment at this

point was allowed, I slammed my door and began pacing

the floor. I could feel myself losing control, and I was

approaching the dark side quickly. I was telling myself,

'it's over now, he is washing up and changing clothes, so

let it go.' After I had calmed down a bit, I headed back

downstairs and went into the diningroom and found my

cousin sitting at the table eating cereal – and still in my

clothes. I turned to the kitchen where my Grandmother

was cooking and said, "Okay enough, do you see that he

still has on my clothes." She responded by yelling, "If you

don't get your ass out of here, you had better!" I remember

screaming and watching my Grandmother's eyes get big

and she got silent. I stormed off and went upstairs and

began digging in the bottom of my closet looking for this

specific boot. (a have always owned lots of shoes, it was a

considerable amount of digging) I returned to the table and

asked once again, "Are you going to take your black ass out

of my shit or…" I was interrupted with the word faggot – I

then went into a rage, and I let the boot have it's way. The

next moments are hazy, I never liked becoming enraged

that way because I can't control that part of me, it's the

point where I have been pushed way too far and I have not

and will not ever apologize for what comes out of that state

because I have darn near begged the person to release me

from their foolishness and at their own discretion they

chose to move forward, Good Luck! The fiasco ended with

broken dishes, milk all over the table, the floor, my cousin

and the china closet behind him. My haze cleared to my

Grandmother yelling in the phone to my Mother that I was

going to make her die of a heart attack, my cousin was

hollering for my Grandmother to get me. My older cousin

was conveying some ridiculousness to my Mother over the

phone about the incident (which he did nothing to prevent,

keep in mind – he is older than my Mother), and when he handed the phone to me all he said, "Your Mom wants you." As he shook his head in disgust of the outcome, which he now had to go clean up for my Grandmother who was now in full Betty Davis mode. My Mother started her ranting and raving for which I basically tuned out, I refused to put any energy into a rebuttal that she wasn't listening to. I was told to bring my ass to her house and stay by myself where I would not be able to be at the cookout. I laughed all the way to her house, it was about a 10 – 15 minute walk, what a joke they all were, did she honestly think I wanted to be around any of them. I was truly forming a strong dislike for the whole group of so called family members. In the days that followed I learned that my cousin was in an argument with some guy at the neighborhood playground and literally came to the house, took my outfit, cut the tags off, went back to the playground and got his ass whipped and drug all over the ground in my new clothes – how much nerve did that take. And it never got addressed!!!!!

What did get addressed one day about a week later when I was at my Mom's house and my cousin was there with a few of his little friends and he become so comfortable with all that he had gotten away with that he let his arrogance lead him into starting in on me right in front of my Mother. And he got to see why it was best to hide like you had been previously. All I did was walk from the kitchen through the livingroom and sat down and he looks at his friends and says, "Little faggot!" I immediately thought, 'This fool had lost his mind,' because it was an unsaid rule, no one in the family had ever pulled that stunt. And in the moments to follow it was evident why not. My Mom's head shot up like a jack-in-the-box as she said, "What did you say?" Arrogance kicked that fool yet again and he responded, "What," just like what he said was okay. She said, "There's nothing wrong with my son." To which he responded, "Are you serious, that boy switches harder than my wife," then had the nerve to look for his friends to chuckle and laugh like they usually do when he floor shows on me, but the only one that didn't catch the shift in the atmosphere of the room was him. Within seconds Miss

Patty – Mother of James Colwell had taken control of the

room and the new punk in the room was her nephew as she

laid down the law about what would be said to her son and

what wouldn't and ended with a promise of missing teeth if

any violations were made. He got the message, and

apologized to her.

About two weeks later as we were all in the kitchen at

my Grandmother's house my cousin decided to inform my

Mom that he did not appreciate me cursing him out. He

was vindictively playing the old game, but new rules had

been put in place and he obviously missed the memo. My

Mother said, "You're right, he has no business talking like

that, he is not grown. But rest a sure he can't argue by

himself and when you start arguing with a 15 year old what

do you expect but for him to talk to you like he talks to 15

year olds." He went on to say, "Patty, I'm not gonna have

him disrespecting me like that." I began to boil, because

this punk was really playing this up like he was such the

adult and I was just out of order for talking back, no matter what he happened to say to me.

This is where I started to know my Mother, the woman – the picture had started becoming clearer to her of some of the things that had been happening and her blinders had come down. Also she had heard a blow by blow version of what went on in that kitchen. The next thing that she said made me know that she has a little bit of clown resting in her psyche. She said, "Listen, this is what you do, at whatever point you feel as though he is disrespecting you and cussing and carrying on, treat him like a man and take him outside and whoop his ass, you have my permission." The kitchen fell quiet, my Grandmother had a very matter of a fact look on her face looking at me (it's a shame because even back then I could tell our relationship was changing.) Then my cousin blurts out, "Now you heard what she said!" I jumped up from the table and said, "I sure did, I heard it like you heard. Now fuck you nigga, let's get it!" I stood at the door waiting to literally tear my cousin's ass out of the frame. He laughed and said, "I ain't

trying to fall out wit my Gram and my Aunt!" Bull crap –
the truth of the matter was at this point I out weighed him
by at least 40lbs and had enough built up anger towards
him that a 911 call would have followed and he knows it.
From that day til this one my cousin and I have not had
another confrontation, GO FIGURE!

Years have soften the feelings that I have toward my
cousin, but I don't give him any space for error, we just
literally don't go down the road of him calling me names or
trying to show off on me. I actually think some maturity
has come into play with him on the subject of me being
different. And in the midst of this I realize yet again, I
really do believe that God has a sense of humor. My first
cousin has three children, and one of them is different.

A coincidence, I think not!

FOUR

<u>Death Of A Legend</u>

I can say without any reservations that I have a Dad that loved me unconditionally, Richard Johnson. He was not my paternal father, but he is the only Dad that I know. I was aware at a very young age that he was not my real father, but I also knew that there was another person who was wasn't around and I gave that individual and their absence no energy. I never had the time to; I spent lots of time with my Dad and equal time with his family. I have a bunch of aunts, uncles and cousins that have always treated me well, there was never a conversation of who belonged and who didn't belong when I was with my Johnson family. I was Richard's oldest child, end of story. My Mom and Dad didn't stay together as a couple for very many years, it was a lot of off and on, but I was never affected by their adult business, my Dad was always around no matter what. As time went on and I grew older my Dad had other girlfriends, all of which, were really good to me and even when they had children of their own with my Dad, their treatment of me was always stellar. I have quite a few siblings from my Dad, they are the best; we even have a set of twins (a boy and a girl) and the funny thing is all my sisters and brothers look just alike, the girls and the boys. They all look just like our Daddy.

I don't have what you would call a close relationship with all of my siblings, but I do have close relation to the children of my Dad's last partner, Alaine. We do keep in touch and I have a beautiful nieces and nephews. Alaine was to my knowledge, the longest lasting mate that my Dad had, other than my Mom. We spent so much time together and she was so involved in my life that I began to call her Mom very early into her and my Dad's relationship and still do to this day. She is my Stepmom and I wouldn't trade her or my siblings for anything. When my Dad wasn't available for a birthday or some landmark thing that I was experiencing, Alaine was Johnny-on-the-spot to cover his part in his absence. Being a parent myself at this point, I understand the commitment to him that she carried and the sacrifice endured by her to make certain that I wasn't affected by my father's absence, while making sure her children were okay as well. I love and appreciate all that she has done throughout the years and always will.

Richard Johnson was a very passionate man when it comes to family and family life. He had his own ideas of what family was supposed to look like and how child rearing was supposed to go and he never broke away from those ideas. He really didn't take any stuff from anyone, if he disagreed with anything that someone was doing, they were going to know about it. Daddy was a small man in stature but he could stand alongside any giant that you could find. I remember one time in particular, when I graduated from the 8th grade my Grandmother was planning a cookout the very next day. About three or four days before she had begun to say to people that it was in celebration of my graduation, but it wasn't true at all. The cookout had been planned well in advance in honor of my

first cousin returning home from jail. Me being me, I
immediately corrected my grandmother and informed her
that, I had never been given a party or dinner in honor of
my birthday or anything (which was something that took
place all the time at our house) and I would have nothing to
do with this ridiculous collaboration. I also let her know
that I felt it was like a slap in my face, with all the work
that I had done versus all he had done was pay his debt to
society for his wrong doings. There was no comparison.
And also, how could it be a party for me, when I have not
one single solitary invited guest, really. She basically
brushed me off in her normal curt way, saying, "Go sit your
ass down somewhere!" And that's exactly what I did, I
went into her bedroom where I planned to spend the rest of
the day. I would not be subject to such foolishness, even if
they didn't realize how foolish and hurtful it really was.
Later on as the guests started to arrive I went downstairs to
get a drink and that's when I seen it and the fur began to
fly. In the center of the table with the rest of the desserts
was the one thing that I asked my Mother for as a gift for

my graduation, a German chocolate cake with chocolate

icing that said, 'Happy Graduation Shaft!'

I took off top speed to the yard to find my Grandmother,

she was just grinning and talking to folks when I came up

to her, she could tell right away that I was pissed, she said,

"What the hell is your problem?" To which I responded,

"In the house, now!" I stormed back in the house and

momentarily she followed. Once in the kitchen we had

words about why she would take my personal gift to serve

her friends and family, she basically came up with a

conclusion that there was nothing I could do about it. I

informed her that I would stomp on it before I allowed it to

happen. She told me, "I wish you would, and I'll beat your

ass!" To which I told her, "Today is the day we are all

gonna keep our promises then, isn't it!" She went back

outside and I went upstairs with my cake in hand and called

my Dad to tell him what happened, all I expected was for

him to calm me down and then later on he would fill my

Mom in on what happened and then my Mom would speak

to my Grandma. But, in a twist of events, my Dad got

furious and said, "What did you say! I'll be there in a minute." And he hung up. Well I got very nervous, because no one challenges my Grandmother. But today was her day. Within about twenty minutes my Dad pulled up out front and pulled me and my Grandma to the side, he was very respectful at first as she told him that I was being smart mouthed and I couldn't tell her what kind of party to throw and what to serve at her house. I watched as his eyebrow raised and he told her, "As long as you stay black don't you ever take anything that House (nickname he called my Mom) buys my son and give it to nobody, and I don't care who's house you at!" And that was it, it was one of the first times I think I've ever seen my Grandma agree to disagree. There was no further arguing and to my knowledge the two of them never revisited that conversation again. I believe my Grandmother knew that she had crossed a lane that she had no business and he just truly wasn't having it. We left, with my cake and I spent the whole day with my Dad and my cousins at my Aunt Sue's (one of his sisters) house and had a great time.

I have many great memories of and with my Dad, he is the one that sparked my crazy obsession with amusement parks and rollercoasters. I have vivid memories of going to West View Park with my dad often; it was the best fun. As soon as I turn the bend to descend into what is now West View Shopping Plaza, I get warm feelings and sometimes even déjà vu of the amusement park that used to occupy that space. The park is gone now and so is my Legend, he passed away when I was in my mid-twenties, but he will never be forgotten. It brings tears to my eyes and chokes me up to know that a man could love a child the way that my Dad loved me, knowing that, that child does not have one drop of your blood racing through it's veins, it is a phenomenal dynamic and a true testimony to who he was as a man. I love you Daddy!

FIVE

<u>Home Away From Home</u>

I've always had another place that I could go to have a break from some of the drama at my Mom's house and my Grandma's place, and that was with my Godparents. No matter where they lived I've always spent time with my Godparents and siblings. I have two Godsisters and one Godbrother, they are actually a lot older than me, but the age difference never really got in the way; I was always closer with my Godsisters. When they lived across town my sisters would come over to my side of town on the bus and pick me up; I would go back with them and stay all weekend and they would bring me back on Sunday. It was some of the best times; by the time I turned 7 my Godparents and siblings had moved to my side of town and I was literally walking distance from them. I spent a lot of time with them in my youth, I always connected the most with my youngest Godsister who happened to be 10 years older than me. She was and can still be one of the funniest people you have ever met. She was so silly and willing to play games with me and we would spend a lot of time watching television and cracking up at the silliest things. We have actually done this in our adult life as well, we both still have wicked senses of humor and get tickled at some of the same things and we would break into laughter until we literally would be dropping tears. My older Godsister is more serious being, she always seemed to be moving at the correct rate to being an adult. She wasn't what I would call stuffy, but the fact is, she was a lot older and that's what she portrayed – a big sister. I always looked up to her more and would rely more on her judgment for things that mattered. She played games and such too, but it was just different, even our conversation topics were different than my younger Godsister. And I know it for a fact now as an adult, I have a more productive relationship with her. One example of that is that my older Godsister and I have never had a shouting match or disagreement that has gone to a level that wasn't becoming. We have a mutual respect for each other, she doesn't disrespect me and I have never disrespected her. The same stood true for my Godbrother, we have never actually gotten into any kind of altercation – he is actually older than all of us, and he was always doing his own thing. The one thing we did share in common is a love for music, so we could talk extensively in that area, it use to tickle him how much I know about music artists and the maturity of my music choices. Things that I wasn't sure on he would clear up for me – he had the whole DJ'ing thing going, he would have all the latest music, and sometimes he played things for me before the radio was even playing them. Those are some really good memories that I have of my Godbrother, those times were cool, especially because I didn't have any positive interactions with my other closely related male cousins. We only had one uncomfortable interaction when I was about 9 years old, and as I've gotten older and reflect back on the memory, I realize that the situation was orchestrated by my youngest Godsister with malicious intent. Both Godsisters and myself were sitting in my Godbrother's bedroom along with him and his girlfriend at the time, my youngest Godsister decided to bring up an awkward subject. She just out of the blue, asked my Godbrother why he didn't spend more time with me and take me places with him. He pretty much try to dance around her questions, but she wouldn't let up until he finally responded, "Why, I can't take him anywhere, it's like having one of your sisters with you. If he acted more like a boy, but naw I aint takin' him nowhere wit' me!" The comment hurt my feelings a bit, but it didn't really matter because I never longed to go anywhere with him anyway, but at that young age it wasn't a good feeling to realize that someone felt that way about you. And how rude is it to speak about a person in that way, just as if they were not in the room. The truth of the matter is, he was crude but my Godsister already had some idea of what her brother's feelings were on the subject and she didn't have to force this dialogue in my presence. But this episode, along with many more to follow, were orchestrated to be hurtful to me. As far as the relationship between my Godbrother and I, it did suffer, our interactions became very short and meaningless and they still are. It is mostly, hello and how have you been, and not much more than that.

My youngest Godsister was a bit of what I would call, a huntress. She would set her sights out on people and then she would attack, it was normal behavior in their house for her. Her older sister was usually the target and as the years went on it was me who started to catch her wrath. It was weird to me to see her actions, because it would come out of nowhere, everything would be going great and she would just switch up mid-stream and all hell would break loose. When she was showing off for other people, I would just chalk it up to her being ridiculous and acting like others in my immediate family. But when she would go into those strange behaviors for no background reason at all, I realized at an early age that there were some issues there, and they were all hers. She would say to me a lot of times, "You're always up here tryna take my spot!" And boy the mistreatment would start. By the time I was 8, the ugly F-word had entered her arsenal of insults. How could this be, I left home trying to get away from this, how could it have followed me here too? It got so bad that I didn't even have to go up to their house for the abuse to go on. I would speak on the phone just about everyday to my Godmother, and when times were good I spent hours on the phone laughing and talking with my youngest Godsister, she didn't have many friends and the few she had didn't spend much time with her. When she would be in her moods and I would call to the house to speak to my Godmother, as soon as she heard my voice she would hang up on me (this is before the days of caller id) – sometimes it took up to three days to get my Godmother on the phone. By the time I was 10 the telephone attacks became brutal, obscenities and homosexual innuendo was being blurted into the phone receiver before the hang up took place. At this time she was 20 and had a child of her own – her behavior was completely inappropriate. There were things that were said that I had no idea what the relevance was, but I was sure that the meaning wasn't anything good. One of her favorite things to say was, "You nasty fag, you just want someone to stick you up your nasty butt!" I didn't have a clue what the significance of that action was. Strangely enough, my Godmother was aware of the situation, and she did nothing. I could never understand why she didn't intervene; I knew she wouldn't choose sides to keep from building on the apparent jealousy issues. Very strange I'd say, being as though, one of us was an adult. It used to go through me like a sharp knife when my Godmom would say, "Yall need to stop that." Meanwhile she knew who was at the center of the problem and watched the whole situation transpire. Though I understand why she chose her position in our ongoing feud, and I have never agreed with her choices, dealing in truth and calling my Godsister out on acting her age, I believe would have brought more positive outcomes. She was never held accountable for her bad behavior and eventually when I was 15 we did have a physical altercation and I could tell that my Godmother was a little pissed at me. It was a ridiculous dynamic, a 25 year old woman with two children physically fighting with a 15 year old child makes no sense. My Mother wasn't very happy with that little situation and I couldn't understand at the time, why she took such offense to it. But once I became a parent and I thought back to this, and I get it.

The truth of the matter is, my Godsister is a 'Convenient Homophobe.' The only way I can explain it is, when it comes to me, she can't help herself from wanting to be in my presence, but there is that one piece of my being that basically makes her cringe. I know how that sounds; it sounds crazy – and that's because **IT IS!!!!!**

I've learned over the years to pretty much ignore a lot of her behavior because quite honestly I don't think she really knows how foolish a lot of her actions are. Some things I believe she could stand to really talk to someone about, it goes a lot deeper than me. From conversations that we have had in the past few years I venture to say that she at one time was bit by the 'Down Low' bug and as a young woman she wasn't about to pull herself out of that space of hurt, and I truly believe, even though it had nothing to do with me personally, that I have been the target to catch the backlash of her shame and anger for all these years. I remember the actual shift in her treatment of me was at a time when she had moved out on her own and things didn't quite go right and she ended moving back home, when she returned, she had this new love/hate thing for me. She has apologized for some of her actions in the last few years, but within that time she has shown other signs that her homophobia of convenience is still alive and thriving. She came clean on breaking toys of mine – when I was around 8 or so, everytime I would spend the weekend with them my Godmom would give me $5.00 when I got there on that Friday, I would immediately go down to the bottom of the hill and buy comic books and a Bat n' Ball. My Godmom would always fuss about the waste of money because the Bat n' Ball would always break by midday on Saturday, and I would always tell her it's nothing that I'm doing, I had them at home too and they didn't break. Well my Godsister admitted to me in 2011 that when I was sleeping she used to take a razor blade and slice on the rubber band that held them together, and the next day after a few rounds it would break. She said she didn't think boys should be playing with that. Still in 2011 she couldn't explain what was the issue with a paddle, a ball and a rubberband, it's the same basis as ping pong. This kind of vindictive behavior being targeted by an 18-19 year old mother to someone elses 8 year old child, I feel is therapy worthy. There were other strange things, such as when teaching each of three children about 'stranger danger' I have witnessed her telling the children that, "You better not get snatched, because a man will snatch you and do it to you in your butt!" Each boy had the same reaction, they didn't know what the hell she meant. I'm sure the comment was for my benefit, but all it did was water the seed that I already had growing that told me, she could stand a little couch time.

Eventually this ongoing foolishness resulted in a separation of me and my extended family, shortly after my high school graduation an episode took place and I vowed to my Godmother that if she would continue to allow her to carry on like she had in the past, that I would just not come into their house, to which she responded, "You're just upset right now James Colwell." I left that day and never stepped foot back in their house for almost the next four years. I wasn't mad at my Godmother, I had just had enough and I just didn't call and I would see her whenever I would run into her at a family function or Bingo. I had adapted so thoroughly to my life without my extended family that my Mother literally had to make me invite my Godmother to my graduation ceremony from Clarissa School of Fashion. My Mom kept asking are you sure you're not mad at her, I assured her I wasn't, and I did extend an invitation, and my Godmother did show up. Eventually we came back together as a family and things were pretty smooth for a long time, though it was due to me ignoring a lot of things as usual. Eventually another separation took place for about four years in 2007, and in that time my Godfather passed away. I was literally told of his death by another family member over the phone as I got of work and stood in the parking lot, and he had already been dead for two days.

Once I ended up joining my church in 2011 and began counsel with my pastor she immediately addressed family relationships and their importance, she went straight for the passing of my Godfather and how it was handled. I agreed to the waste of energy that was being used and mended the fence with my extended family – yet again it has proven to be an interesting farse where it concerns my youngest Godsister and her eldest son. Out of nowhere, her son decided to go into a rant and stated that I am not his Uncle nor am I her Brother or Godbrother; I am just their cousin. This blindsided me, naturally, this child has referred to me all of his life as his Uncle, and now after 30+ years he was carrying on and basically denouncing me with such venom that it didn't make any sense. This all took place while my Godsister and I were on the phone, he knew that I was on the other end and I could hear him and trust me his comments were made with definite and intentional venom. He and I had never had a cross word before that day, I didn't understand – but immediately after the initial shock, I didn't care to understand. Several weeks later, my Godsister told me her son sent a message of apology, to which I declined and told her to tell my cousin, that we are cool, just like that and the bell can't be unrang.

Then there are times where my Godsister is just playing ignorant while all along carrying the intention to be offensive – such as making comments like, "Oh, I thought all gay people loved to suck dick." Over the years I have explained to her that is absolutely not true, but she will bring it up again and again and say, "You know I don't know, you gotta explain that stuff to me." The last time she tried this passive aggressive tactic, I attacked back just as nonchalantly and asked her do all females smell like fish a few days a month. Of course she became very offended and defensive. To which I gave her flighty act right back to her and said, "You know I don't know, I thought yall did." She replied, "You know better than that." I just shrugged my shoulders.

It really is disturbing how you can have such issues with a lifestyle and the people in it, but can't help yourself from throwing yourself into their space. Everytime the LOGO Channel runs a Noah's Arc Marathon, she is glued to the television set – why does she even subscribe to LOGO, she pays money monthly to have access to that channel; again that's the road leading to a straight-jacket. It really is something to witness how a person will play both sides of the fence, literally she had to be one of the biggest fans when I released my Loving Topaz Series of books in 2011-2012. She can speak to you about the characters, maybe better than me – due to the fact that she has read all three books multiple times. She has lent her books to other people on job to read and she is always talking about Topaz like he is a real person and arguing with me about plot decisions that I've made, to the point that I would tease her by calling her the woman from Stephen King's Misery novel – and guess what, that broad was truly coo-coo for Cocoa Puffs too. There is no disguising the fact that the Topaz character is a 16 year old openly gay male and his interaction with other characters in the books are an almost mirror image to my interaction with her over the years. She has such compassion for the fictional character that it is almost disturbing.

More disturbing is the fun that we have when none of the crazy is in the picture and I believe that is why I have always tried to work out the relationship but it just gets to a point where I'm not going to sacrifice who I am for any relationship. And I won't be a punching bag for anyone, no matter how much they claim they're not punching me. Comments like, "Oh, I like you so much better, with your walk with Christ!" And when I addressed the fact that I found that offensive, she played the game and swore, "Oh no you're taking it the wrong way." But after that instance, she would continue to make that comment and would just ignore her, then one day she said it in the presence of another person who flat out asked her, "Are you serious, that wasn't a nice thing to say to anyone." She then preceded to try to convince that person that they took it the wrong way as well. The visitor told her she could explain it anyway that she wants but it sounds like you are saying you like him now that he goes to church and you didn't like him before. And I told the visitor, "I told her the same thing." Later that day my Godsister tried to flip the script and said that the visitor was a troublemaker and she didn't want to be in the presence of her again, because Heaven is her goal and people like that were not of God. I just laughed and thought to myself, 'There goes the crazy rearing it's ugly head again.'

Our last episode was basically when I decided to do this book, she got upset and told me it was not necessary and I needed to be writing more Topaz books. She then asked me if I was going to put her in the book, I said, "Are you kidding, you played a part in a large portion of my life." She did tell me at that time, "Shaft, if there is anything that you feel that I have ever done to you, I'm really sorry."

I said, "Okay," I laughed and said, "Don't worry about it, because…Ultimately, whatever you did, was what you wanted!" Shortly after that she stopped speaking to me. Hilarious.

SIX

<u>Death Of An Icon</u>

I have had the distinct pleasure of coming into direct contact with my own personal icon. He was a strange man, a creative man, a stern man, a giving man, a family man and most important of all, he was my Godfather.

His name was James George. Which as a child I always thought was as unique as he was, he had two first names. My Godfather was a very quiet person who pulled no punches, he was brutally honest most times. He took no crap from anyone and he didn't have friends and didn't make friends easy, over the years he would open up to me to explain why he was the way he was and why his thought process was the way it was. The thing that stood out is that my Godfather had no relationship with any of his family. He didn't like to go into details about it but what I gathered is, his childhood wasn't the best and he was not a very forgiving person at all. He believed what people say and do are their truth and you need to listen to people when they are speaking and take them for their word. I remember him saying to my Godmother one day, "Helen, you need to pay attention to what people say and believe that, that is what they mean, period!" That comment has stayed with me all these years and my Godfather was absolutely correct. It is to your best interest to take people at their word.

Another thing my Godfather would share with me was the friendship he shared with my Mom. He would always say how much he liked her, because she was different than the rest of my family, he would say that she was genuine and the rest of my family wasn't. As the years strolled by I would find that once again Jim George was absolutely correct. My Godfather was a very giving man if he cared about you or believed in you. He loved me before I was even born, so much so, that he gave me his first name, and my Mom agreed. It is such a special honor to carry his name, because he never had any paternal children of his own. He was married to my Mom's cousin and that is how

I got my Godmother. My Mom always says, "It was

natural that Helen would be your Godmother; she's

Jimmy's wife. And she has been a damn good

Godmother." The funny thing is that my Godmother's

sister, (who is naturally our cousin as well. I refer to her as

Aunt Barb) happened to have a closer relationship with my

Mom, they hung out together, where as my Godmother

hung out with my mother's sister (they are closer in age).

Aunt Barb would always tell my Mom and my Godmom

whenever she got a chance, "He should've been my

godchild, I'm the one that was with her through the whole

pregnancy, running back and forth to the hospital!" I

remember her saying that as far back as I can remember,

she wouldn't let it go, so I would venture to say that the

decision my Mom made hurt Aunt Barb's feelings. My

Mom has apologize a ton of times for that, and once I

became of age and understood what it was about, I always

made sure to tell my Aunt Barb how I felt about her. Aunt

Barb was an absolute favorite of mine, she was so much

fun and always had a unique way of expressing herself. She was a very petite woman with natural red hair and freckles and an extensive vocabulary of curse words. Oh boy, did she know how to curse a person out, and she didn't mind doing it. She past away a few years before my Godfather, and I miss her like crazy.

My Godfather was the most introverted person that I have ever met, I swear that man didn't use ten words in a day sometimes. He was also one of the most talented people that I have ever come in contact with. My Godfather was a very skilled artist, he watched television and he drew pictures of women who always appeared to be strong, a lot of the pictures remind me of gorgeous African-American amazons. I am very sad that I never asked him for any of those drawings, I don't know what my Godmother did with them, there had to be thousands of them. I do have a huge backdrop that he painted for a competition that I took part in and the easel he built from scratch to accommodate the backdrop. And I have all of the lessons and tips that over the years he gave me. My

Godfather realized early on that I had artistic talent and he jumped right into action with teaching me the proper way to sketch and the importance of proportion and proper shading, etc. Those are skills that I use almost everyday of my life and memories that no one can ever take away.

Could he be a little intimidating at times, sure he could. But it was more a thing for me of not wanting to disappoint him. The one thing that sticks out in my mind that defines solely how my Godfather was and what he felt about me is this one particular day when I was visiting. My Godmother and I were playing backgammon and discussing different things that were going on with me, as I was in my early twenties at this point and owned my own home. I revealed to her that I was very uncomfortable with the fact that I had never had a conversation with my Godfather about my sexuality and I had no clue on his feelings about it. I told her that I had talked to my Dad about it and he had no problem with it, and laughed at me for thinking that he would have a problem. We had moved on to a completely different subject when my Godfather came downstairs and went into the kitchen, my Godmother got up and went into the china closet that sat in the diningroom where we were, I paid her no attention, nothing was out of the ordinary. She sat back down and continued playing, as my Godfather walked back through the diningroom to go back upstairs, she stopped him and said, "Jimmy," he turned around and approached the table she laid a promo picture of me in full drag on the table in front of him and said, "Do you know who that is?" I was mortified, I was worried about the sexuality issue and now she has thrown the drag issue on top of it, I was just horrified. He picked the picture up without flinching and said, "Helen are you serious, what would make you think that I don't know my Godson when I see him! The boy is named after me." I was shocked, but I felt relieved. He went on, "He's good at whatever he tries, and that's what always counted." He took his items that he had gathered from the kitchen and went upstairs and the subject of sexuality was never brought up between us again.

My Godfather passed away when I was in my mid-thirties, leaving a void that no other person can fill. He was nothing less than an Icon in my life.

THE WORLD

IS A

DIFFERENT

KIND OF PLACE

SEVEN

<u>Family vs The World</u>

By the age of 9 I knew that there was something about me that was definitely different than everyone that I was around, the truth was it wasn't just sexuality, I absolutely had nothing in common with my family. I couldn't actually identify with one member of my immediate of family or my extended family, I just had a completely different thought pattern. And then there was the obvious difference that I had with other little boys, it was weird for everyone else, it has never bothered me, I never wanted to be a carbon copy of anyone. This was a good thing I feel as I look back on it all, I had no identity issues because I was always free to and willing to express myself. I had already begun to build a tough skin before I ever got to school age, so I wasn't blind sided by the bullying and name calling, it's a shame but it was already becoming my normal. As an adult when I talk about some of my adolescence with my Mom, she asks me, "If things were so bad in a place why would you go back, you weren't made to go to these places." I then explained to her, this was a large part of what went on everywhere I went, it was pretty much, the norm. I didn't even have to do anything to get it started, just show up. And when I say everywhere, that's what I mean, my Mom's house, my Grandmother's house, my cousin's houses, my Godparent's house, the playground, the school, and on and on. I could literally be walking to the store and someone would yell, "Faggot!" from a car window, or a house window and then duck there head back in, I've always thought that the behavior was idiotic, and cowardly. Why throw a rock and hide your hand? Stand in your dirt. To tell the truth, there wasn't very much that could be said to hurt my feelings out in the world, for I had hear if all at home. You would have to come up with something more creative if you wanted to get me rattled.

When people would ask me in my adolescence if I was gay, I would reply, "No." And the funny thing is as far as I was concerned, that was true. I wasn't anything but, James. I wasn't attracted to anyone, my hormones were late kicking in, and I believe it was do to so much other turmoil swirling in my life, that was the last thing I was thinking about. I knew that I was different in the early years, when everybody was looking for boyfriends and girlfriends, I didn't want a boyfriend, but I knew that I definitely didn't want a girlfriend. All of that running around collecting folks' phone numbers, just seemed so silly to me. I never had an actual strong feeling of physical attraction toward another person until I was 16, which was the summer before I started my senior year of high school. Which also happened to be the same time I began my journey to learn to sew and design clothing. Trust me when I tell you, patterns, fabric and thread won out over strange feelings and urges – my creative genes always win over my animalistic ones. I remember the day that my hormones kicked in just like it was yesterday, it was a summer day and I was standing in our kitchen looking out of the large sliding glass doors that are between me and the side porch outside. There were several of the guys playing football in the street, like they always did, I never found it interesting and this day was no different. The game was uneventful as were the players except this one, for some reason I couldn't figure out why I kept staring at him, it was the weirdest thing, I had gone to school with him everyday for the past three years and I hadn't paid him all that much attention. I mean, I wasn't crazy, I thought he was cute but that was as far as it went. And at this time I had experienced plenty of indecent proposals that I had no interest in. For whatever reason, today I was checking him out like one of the Twilight vampires, I took in his whole essence and I had him on lock just as if I was hunting prey. After I realized over thirty minutes had gone by, I had to laugh at myself for almost being in stalker mode, or was I. I figured out later that evening what that rush of emotions was. These moments were a little tough, because I literally had no one to talk them over with, and no one to warn me what was coming. I think in some ways it is for the best that I had to

figure out my adolescence alone, because I was slow on the

trigger, and I was clueless of what I was shooting at. I

know for a fact that when I did give up my virginity five

years later to a older guy from the other side of town, I

wasn't led by fear, ignorance or peer pressure. It was

simply my time, and I was old enough to make an informed

decision. I have to say, not being really friendly with the

guys my own age probably did help me in that weakened

state on that summer day at the age of 15, because had we

been having some type of dialogue or rapport, ole boy

would've probably been able to talk me into anything. It

was truly a hot day and the air conditioners were not taking

care of my heat. Lord knows, a Singer sewing machine

saved me and kept my virtue in tact for another 5 years.

My growing up as a **DIFFERENT** teen left me on many

occasions feeling like I was 'lonely in a crowded room.'

Truly that's the feeling I carried around most of the time,

I've always enjoyed my alone time; me and my music and

my crafts, there truly wasn't enough hours in the day. I am

most comfortable when I am alone. There are very few times that I feel that I am a part of a group or unit. I always feel like it is me and I am with all the other people, I remember feeling this at all gatherings growing up, while going through old pictures, I see myself and my own birthday parties and I look like a guest. This is something that I must work on myself, because I still experience this feeling today at age 41.

There are very few times and people that I feel close enough to let my guard down with, and sometimes I simply can't, it just is what it is. When it would be just me and my Grandmother one on one I felt completely engaged, the same thing with my Mother. But the strangest thing is when a conversation is involving my Mother and my Brother, I become the outsider, it's the weirdest thing, I always feel as though I am sitting in on their conversation, it use to bother me, but it doesn't anymore, I know for sure that it's nothing that they are doing, they just really do have more in common. Two facts that I can openly state are...

I know that my Mother and my Brother love me

unconditionally. My Mother is who she is and she is the

only family member that I have to date that has always

stood in her truth no matter how anybody felt and what was

said. She stated early in my adulthood that she is not happy

with the fact that I am gay, it is not her choice for me and

she is only going to be comfortable with so much of my

lifestyle in her presence. And as time has gone on, that

comfort level has grown tremendously. Her comfort level

is tested when it comes to love interests, and we just do not

approach that. I respect her and the fact that she is honest

about her feelings and I go out of my way to keep her

comfortable, within reason with the things that I can

control. An example of that is, early on, when I was in my

twenties I did work as a licensed cosmetologist and my

hairstyle was forever changing. This use to drive my

Mother crazy, to the point where she said to me, "You are

not going anywhere with me with your hair like that." Well

there was no argument or debate, I told her to have a great

day and I kept it moving. This was not in reason, it was

extremely self-centered and obnoxious, my take on it is that she was worried about other people's thoughts, and that is unacceptable. Another example is, I know she has an issue with the whole dating and love interest situation; I dated the same guy for roughly eight and a half years and he has only been in my Mother's presence three or four times, for no longer than a fifteen minute period. I had no problem with this, he was dating me, not her and there wasn't any pressing reason that either one of them had to be put in a position of discomfort. Now as far as my Brother is concerned, there is no conversation needed that involves my sexuality, he will not even entertain dialogue with people about it, he doesn't find it necessary. There was an instance when he was around 16, where a family member and a few of their children basically ambushed him and tried to drill him on his feelings about my sexuality and how it made him feel. He let them know politely that they were out of order, and not to ever cross that bridge again. The second fact is when it comes to verbal abuse and hurt feelings, the World had no chance to place it's mental scar on me; my Family had assured that all of my scars were in place by the time I entered second grade.

EIGHT

<u>Growing Pains</u>

As the world continued to spin on it's axis I continued to receive my life lessons and uppercuts. I had no idea at the time but my skin was getting tough and I was being equipped to deal with the near future. I could never grasp why the constant ridicule was so necessary, but it seemed that my older cousins got off on it. I suppose this is a normal thing for older cousins and siblings to pick on younger ones, but the orchestration that was used by some of my cousins was more personal and detailed than most of what they would eventually accomplish in their adult lives.

I have a female cousin who happens to be around six years older than me; she has actually been trusted with keeping an eye on myself and the younger cousins in the past. Before I go any further, let me explain the age differences in myself and my cousins. There is my one male cousin who is nine months younger than me, he and I basically sit alone in the middle. We have cousins that are three to five years younger than us and then there are cousins that are five to ten years older than us. Now as I was saying, this female cousin was interesting, she wasn't necessarily mean at first, but that changed as I got older and it was evident that I wasn't one to roll over and play dead. So our interactions weren't always great growing up, any type of altercation was always blamed on me and she would be especially groovy if it involved her younger sibling or her first cousins (yes, they were my second cousins). This was the case a lot of times, though I've always liked my younger cousin who was her brother, but he was the baby of their family and a total brat, and the rest of the cousins were pretty much prone to eat a mile of his shit. It never flew with me, and he knew it. But the fact that I wouldn't bow to the so-called King, made me a target at times. When I was 11 years old all of the younger cousins and neighborhood children that were playing with us on that summer day were instructed by my now 16 year old cousin to stop calling me Shaft. This came as it always did, there was an altercation with myself and her younger brother, to which she watched go down and my little cousin was out of order, as usual. Before it escalated to a physical, which is where we fast approaching, she intervened by standing on the porch and calling the attention of everyone and saying, "Shut up faggot, you are always starting. Y'all stop calling him Shaft, that's not his name his name is Shafina, and that's what y'all call him from now on." Of course this gained a good laugh all the way until I gave her one good swift, "Fuck you!" But the instruction was successful for most of that summer, I was taunted and called Shafina but it cost them, there were few of those children that didn't get slapped in their mouths that summer, and they could all thank her for that. The cute part is that my mother was told that I cursed at her for no reason at all. Sometimes there were things done to cover one's own pain and struggle, but that doesn't make it right. As an adult I am a little more understanding about certain things, but to be drug through the mud because of someone else embarrassment is rough. Just as what went on with my

Godsister and her unresolved issues about homosexuality,

this female cousin was harboring some of her own. She has

a sibling with the exact same affliction, he is no different

than me. He is and was as gay as a three dollar bill. The

funny thing is he had the nerve to be one of the cousins that

hung with my first cousins and antagonized me horribly,

when all along – doing some man-touching of his own.

Once I realized that he was gay, it was many years later and

I was really disappointed to know that someone would be

so self-indulgent and ultimately to a family member. I

could have handled it better if he would have just hid in his

closet and let the spot light shine where it may, but for you

to literally push me out on center stage and give input to the

abuse. Well that truly is what a FAGGOT is!

These types of episodes flooded my childhood, looking

back it is amazing that I even speak to or have relationships

with any of my family members. A lot of things have been

forgiven under the grounds of growing up and maturing,

but the truth of the matter is a lot of what was done to me

was done at an age where these folks knew exactly what they were doing and they have made nice and apologetic in the later years because there is something in their mind to gain by being on good terms with me. The cute part is that they don't think that I realize it.

This constant back and forth did take it's toll on me as a youngster, I began to fight a lot, and it spilled over to my school life. My patience grew shorter as I grew older and it turned into folks trying to psychoanalyze me without my permission. I got tired of hearing, "Oh he has a chip on his shoulder!" and "He is mean, and he tries to hurt people before they get the chance to hurt him!" I realized that adults in a school setting couldn't just come out and say, 'This child is gay and I don't know how to help him.' Or possibly, 'I don't want to help him.' So things quickly spiraled into a situation where I was looked at like a snap-out or a bad kid, and this was so far from the truth. I ended up in an abundance of suspensions for fighting and cursing folks out. I never really understood the gay-bashing thing until many years later. It was very disturbing to me, I cannot understand how some of those people could endure the physical abuse the way they did. I couldn't even stand too much of that lip action and it was a full out fight going on.

When I was in 6th Grade I wound up going to St. James Catholic School for a year, and it was the most ridiculous experience ever. That school wasn't ready for my quick hit methods, they believed in talking things over and paddling. It didn't take long before I let them know that I was interested in giving out ass-whoopings and not receiving them. After being there for close to a year, I ended up being placed twice a week with a psychologist that was located around the corner from the school and I would go there mid way through the day and all he did was play Uno and ask me why do I get angry? He didn't have any advice other than, ignoring the mistreatment of others. I said I would give it a shot. I was doing well with ignoring folks, but dying on the inside because I was really wanting to hurt a few of them. It all came to a head the one day when I came back to school after missing a day due to a dental appointment. No sooner than I boarded the school bus I

was told of some disturbing comments that were said by a

nun at the school that was an English teacher. As we got to

the school I heard the same things in breakfast and two or

three other times throughout the day. At first I was just

going to ignore the kids until the constant telling of the

exact story. Sister Zachary was my final period of the day,

the ill feelings had stewed within me all day, coupled with

the fact that she never treated me very well and it was

evident. Once I reached her class, I took my seat and right

before she got started I raised my hand and said, "Sister

Zachary, I was informed by my classmates of what I

missed yesterday and I wanted to make sure that I didn't

miss anything." She said, "Okay, and what did they tell

you we did." I said, "Well the first thing was that you

addressed the whole class and asked where was the class

fairy today." Her eyes got kind of big, and I went on, "Is

this true or are these Christian students lying?" She then

said, "Well where were you yesterday." At that time, I

took one big deep breath and cussed her out for the next ten minutes until she sent someone for the principal. The next day when I returned to my therapist's office, I told him exactly what I thought of his advice and informed him that I would not be returning to his office again, no matter what the school said. And he should try some other profession because his counsel was bullshit. Within the next weeks my Mom changed my school.

I was presented with the therapy farse once again in high school, this time it was a well-known Muslim gentleman from my own neighborhood. I think his role was more of a counselor of sorts at Langley High School. We only had one session, and it was an epic fail. He started by asking me why I am so angry and having these problems that prompted the school to involve him. I proceeded to explain to him some of the triggers that makes me snap at the other students and staff. His solutions were as follows…

Can't you try to copy one of the boys' walks around school instead of your own walk. And try to talk with your voice in a lower tone.

I realized right away that he was even more clueless than the Caucasian man that I wasted my time with in middle school. I promptly told him, "Let's stop this now, because I have always liked and respected you and if we keep talking that's going to change. You don't know how to help me and you're not being fair to me or yourself. You are a Muslim and I know that respect is a huge thing with you. And I'm telling you, I will never change me to make someone else comfortable. And I'm never going to accept people disrespecting me." I got up and excused myself and never returned to his office.

Shortly after this I fought a bit of a bought with depression, things at school weren't getting any better, home life was continuing to be brutal as it had been. Some of the things that I hadn't understood previously were starting to make sense and it was getting to be a lot to handle. Before I knew it I was dealing with choices of suicide. It was just a simple as the fact that I'd had enough, and I seen no light at the end of the tunnel. I had it all planned out, my Grandmother would be going out on that particular weekend and I would be home alone with my Great-Grandmother who paid me no attention anyway. I knew where all of my Grandmother's medications were and we always had liquor in the house and it would be seamless, I would take the medications, drink the liquor, go to sleep and alls well that ends well. For whatever reason I had a long talk with my inner-self at around 3 a.m. the day before (as I've gotten older, I realized this was my form of prayer, I always believed that God lived within me-and he does answer you). I came to the conclusion that I was not solving anything by leaving, that the people doing all the button pushing – family and otherwise would actually be winning, and how could I let that happen? I deserved to win in this life, I didn't ask to be here. I haven't done anything to anyone while I've been here. My spot is equally as important as anyone elses, and I was going to do everything in my power to make certain that people knew I had been here.

I have never again been in that dark corner and when I hear anyone even start to sound as though they are contemplating going down that road I jump into action. I don't suggest that anyone work through it the way I did, there are licensed professionals that are a phone call away that can help anyone going through this. I was lucky and God had a plan for me, and that is why I am still here, because there was nothing in between me and those pills but that quiet inner-voice of mine.

The next years to come were when I really started to learn what made me happy and how to really go for it, unapologetically. I accepted that I was different, and it wasn't going to change and why should it. I didn't even understand all of my differences but I would welcome them as they came and I would rush nothing. About a year later, I met my absolute best friend ever, Stephanie Whitely, for which I referred to as Stevie. We were paired together by her Mom, Juanita. I've known her Mom as long as I could remember, they lived up the street from my Grandmother. Juanita worked with my Gram at the Bidwell Training Center, which is now the Manchester Craftman's Guild. I had my first summer job there in 1986 working under

Juanita, by this time my Grandmother wasn't working anymore, she left Bidwell in 1980. Juanita was fabulous and always so nice to me, very motherly at all times, she taught me many things about the world of an Administrative Assistant and Switchboard Operator, she was the best. She would always say, I have to introduce you to my daughter, you two have so much in common you would love her. And in the fall of that year, that's just what she did. Stevie had returned home from college and we met and immediately hit it off, it was a while before we realized that she was 10 years older than I was. But it didn't matter, I loved her and she loved me, she introduced me to a World that would ultimately become mine. She took me to my first Ebony Fashion Fair and I will never forget it, such beauty, drama and glamour. We went to all kinds of fashion shows, hair shows, concerts and talent shows; whatever my interests were, that were age appropriate. And when I became of age she took me to my first cabaret.

And speaking of talent shows, I can never forget the time that I was set to perform in the community day talent show, I was 14 at the time. My cousins and I had been talking about this for weeks and it was finally here. Literally hours before the show, we were down at my cousin's house and no one was doing the show, everyone had chickened out. Well I informed them that I was all ready to go, it was weird because I didn't understand why they were afraid, it's just our community, but now I realize, I could've cared less what the community thought, I was doing this for me. One of my younger cousins went into the house and told the folks in there that I was doing the talent show and out came my female cousin in her normal venomous way, questioning why I wanted to do the talent show and swearing that I was going to embarrass the whole family. I didn't even argue with her, I had plans and they didn't involve her antics. Stevie and I had spoken the day before and she gave me the pep talk of a lifetime and said, "Go for it!" That was all I needed. I changed my clothes and prepared myself to compete and I did. I basically re-

enacted the Janet Jackson Control video, all black outfit
and all. (this was probably the set up for my future as a
performer, and I had no clue) I watched the crowd as I
began performing, it was really quiet, like people were
waiting to see just what the hell was going to happen,
within a minute of the dialogue at the beginning it was all
cheers and shouts for me to do my thang. I ended up being
the winner of the talent show. And it was just a reiteration
of my family and their convenient backing, after the win,
the vibe changed to, "We knew you was gonna throw
down, you tore it up cuz!" Ridiculous. The only praise I
needed was from Stevie, and I had that whether I won or
lost. And oh my goodness we would laugh, she was as silly
as I was and we would laugh until we cried and no one got
the joke but us. She was truly my best friend and the sister
that my Mom didn't give me. She has since past on and so
has her mom, but I know they are angels in heaven
cheering on my every move.

There is another person who grabbed my hand and
introduced me to a whole new part of the World and that

was Riquetta Brown, I refer to her as 'The Other Mother.' And that's just what she is. One of the most beautiful women that you will meet, inside and out, is my Riquetta, she has known me all of my life, but as I reached adulthood she and I bonded like cement forming a completely different relationship than what was there before. She introduced me to the world of Cosmetology and single handedly taught me the proper way to conduct yourself in an adult setting. The dos and don'ts and how to keep a clean reputation and basically carry yourself with class, no matter what else is going on. I have carried these lessons with me all of my adulthood, one that has come in handy is, "No matter how a situation is going with a love interest, you do not scream and yell in the streets, it's just not lady like." Riquetta has three children that are older than me and two that are younger, and I thank them for letting me borrow her from time to time. I think the most important thing that my Other Mother has shared with me is, "No matter what goals you set for yourself, they don't have to make any sense to anyone but you, and everyday is another day to go toward them." Thanks Ma!

NINE

<u>? Friendships ? Respect ?</u>

Friendship is something that requires constant work, just as any other relationship. What I have learned is, it is very important to understand in detail each member of the friendship's intentions and expectations. The worst thing ever is, to find yourself involved in a one sided friendship. I have done this multiple times and it is really not a good feeling. Being a gay male makes this even more important and ultimately necessary to protect yourself from being hurt and/or used. Over my years I have witnessed people who will befriend homosexuals because they think that we are cool, or different. Or they think it makes them look cool and diverse. This is nothing more than a form of use, you deserve to have a true friendship, one that doesn't include you feeling overwhelmed with the requests or the needs of your so-called friend. It is really not hard to figure out when you are in this situation, if you feel used at times or like the only time the friendship isn't rocky is when you are sacrificing – **YOUR IN IT!**

I am ever so guilty of this, and the friendships are not always outside individuals, blood relatives are notorious for this. And they tend to get away with it a lot more because you are family, you are more prone to let them slide on certain things. I am a naturally giving person and this works against me on occasion, if this is your personality type, it is necessary to pull back, at least in the beginning so you know that you are offering yourself to a deserving party.

Honesty is the most important factor in your friendship and boundaries really do help. Sometimes surprises breaks the bond, but if everybody understands what is going on, there is no room for error.

Here is a perfect example…

My best friend was Stephanie Whitely (Stevie) but I was not her best friend and this is something that we discussed openly and freely. This sounds funny but it really is not, for one thing, Stevie was 10 years older than me, so she already had her best friend before we met. And one rule that we followed was, I did not ever attack their friendship or it's dynamic, I let her handle that relationship, it was none of my business. The reason is, I know how I felt about her and I would have told anyone to back off and let me handle our bond. And as a result, my best friend has gone home to glory, and I can say with a smile, we NEVER had a falling out. We were friends for over 20 years and never had a day of not speaking to each other, there are siblings that can't say that, but I can about my dear friend. We weren't perfect, but we knew how to disagree in complete agreement and no one had to give in. She was put in my life for a reason, the timing that she came into my life was strategic and though I miss her terribly, I do not question that plan on my life or hers that God has, I know she is with him causing someone else the happiness that she did me and I just thank him for the time that he gave me with my BEST FRIEND.

I was also granted another beacon of light which was unlikely but for some reason fit right into the puzzle that I call my life. His name is Edward Harper (Chet), and we have a bond that cannot be interrupted by a soul walking this planet, I love him the way that I love Jermaine. I never thought it was possible to feel as strongly about anyone as I do my brother, but then Chet showed up. We are as different as night and day but we just make sense – we are very honest with each other, sometimes brutally, but that works for our dynamic. He will call me on my shit and for some reason, he loves to make fun of me. He thinks I'm a bit overdramatic at times, and it has on occasion brought him to tears through laughter. I remember the day that I met him, I had no intention of creating a friendship with him, but the strange thing is it happened without any effort and I have a hard time remembering when he wasn't around, he fits and that's it. The best thing is, he got to experience time with Stevie and they hit it off and had their own friendship as well. The three of us together is as close to harmony as I can describe. So I can successfully say, lightning does strike in the same spot twice. I have two individuals that God gave me to experience friendship that most people will never know.

I am still learning that there is only one Chet and one Stevie and I cannot open myself up to everyone who crosses my path with a good friendship request. It is very simple, I see the signs and choose to ignore them, trying to give the benefit of a doubt, and when I look up, I'm fed up and then being accused of being mean. A joke right, I know. I've done this over and over with family members and outsiders alike. I let things go way to often, and the more you forgive the worse the people get. A lot of times I have looked back on these situations and found that there is an utter lack of respect that plays a huge part in this.

I am a person that believes I have no control over how you feel about me as a person, just how I allow you to treat me. I know that we all have someone in our lives that you know in your soul, that they feel like they are better than you. And it is generally socially that they feel this way, now I'm going to go as far as saying, the few people that I have this situation with, I pretty much ignore. Because that is their mechanism on how to cope with their broken lives, there's no need to address those feelings, because when they lay down in the evening, the truth lays down with them and they know who I am and they are actually threatened by the fact that we are not equally matched socially, but the odds do not fall in their favor. So there will be small passive aggressive attacks from these people, and it will come in a form that they feel is over your head, and it never is. I always say, just because I'm not screaming and yelling, doesn't mean I don't see you!

If you listen really closely you will hear the facts, truths that explain to you that the respect level that I have for you is low, so whatever I dish you should be willing to take, if you are even smart enough to catch that I am attacking you. I find this behavior most offensive, here is an example of a slight dig in the respect department…

One of my cousins has children that are naturally over 17 years younger than me, needless to say, they are not my peers. Her children refer to me by my first name, although, we were not raised this way, her parents are my cousins as well and I have always referred to them as Aunt and Uncle. We have cousins that are at least three years younger than me and her children refer to them as Aunt and Uncle, which means the family tradition hasn't changed. Now let me say this; this is not a problem, because that is your choice and that has everything to do with how you view me personally. But where the problem lies is when she was trying to gear my children to call her children Aunt and Uncle and meanwhile her Grandchildren are now calling me by my first name. Yes, blatant disrespect! There was no need for an argument about this, because all that would've happened is I would've been told that I was wrong and that wasn't what was going on, because not only am I dense in your eyes, I'm stupid too. I just make sure my children know who to address and who not to address as an aunt or an uncle.

Another situation arose where one of my younger cousin's daughter asked me to be her baby's Godfather and this child was questioned in detail by several family members as to why was I her choice to be the godparent of this child. Are you kidding me, I don't even get why this was being done to her, she was pregnant at the time and definitely didn't need this unnecessary stress. I have two legally adopted children and a Godchild that is now 22 years old, I think I far surpass the qualifications of godparent. So what really is the problem, of course no one had the nerve to contact me and say anything. Again, messiness at it's best, in a whisper.

There is another area of respect in friendship that you must pay close attention to, and it is all on you personally. I've said before, it is essential for you to know what type of friendship you are building. Yes, you are responsible for protecting yourself in your journey of friendship. Let me explain and give an example...

I have an individual for which I had no reason to question that we were great friends. We met in 1993 and this person and I have spent countless number of hours hanging out together we have gone shopping, eating, drinking, shows, movies, you name it. She use to frequent my home several times at week at points. We have shared secrets, tears and many laughs. We have interacted for years with each others family, so much so that I actually named her my youngest child's Godmother when he was born in 2006. And we still speak on the phone or send texts everyday. Strangely enough, we went through a rocky period when she got engaged. I was ecstatic, because this was one of her life goals coming alive right in front of our faces. She always talked about being a wife and a mother, it was her childhood dream. We dove in, into the long journey of the right dress, the right jewelry, etc. I didn't go to all the shopping and such, I was on the other end, once the dress was chosen I did the necessary alterations for her and others in the wedding party, we had fun collaborating on the hair and the make up was all on me, she is a natural girl, so she stayed in her lane and let me worry about that stuff. We have been friends so long that I think she forgets that I'm not one of the girls at times and I get invited to all kinds of stuff – baby showers, sex toy parties, etc. In this case I was even invited to the bachelorette party. Things got hectic as the date approached as it does for most

weddings, there were changes made to the guest lists

amongst other things, one of the changes was my

invitation. I was told that she had to streamline her guest

list and I would not make the list. I had no problem with

this and as a friend, I understood the bottom line is green

and sometimes you have to cut where you can. I didn't

think anymore of it, though other friends and family

members of mine didn't get it. I was on a spree of

upholding the decision that she had made. My feelings

were not hurt, and I rolled with the punches until one day

about three weeks after the wedding when I was throwing a

card party at my house. I didn't invite this individual and

she literally called me and told me off. At first I thought

she was joking, but she wasn't. She was very offended and

she let me know it, she is usually a very laid back person,

but she had it going on this night. Until I said, "What is

really going on," I explained to her that the reason I didn't

extend an invitation was because she doesn't gamble and

doesn't even know how to play cards. She didn't agree and

didn't take it lightly, she told me she could have come and eat and watched television with my baby. To lighten the conversation, I reminded her that I do eat wedding cake and I didn't snap out about not being invited to the wedding. She went on and said that it was different; her exact words were, "I was only able to invite my closest and dearest friends. And I explained that to you." And at that very moment is the first time, honestly that I felt any kind of way about this whole wedding fiasco. Those words cut like a knife, because up to that very moment I thought I was one of those people, but I guess I was wrong. We ended that conversation and moved on, but I had some moments shortly after when I felt like maybe I didn't want to continue on with the friendship, I was very hurt. Then I stepped back and looked at everything and took ownership of what was mine. And that was the dynamic of our friendship, she never said one time that I was one of her closest or dearest friends, that was all in my head. So would it be fair for me to lash out and drop the friendship when the misconception was on my end? The adult in me said no, 'You did this, now deal.' I ate those feelings and said that I would never make that mistake again, that is what life is about, so I moved forward with the individual and left that in the past. It truly helped when we ran into another little patch about a year later when she gave birth to her first child and ran into an issue about naming godparents for the baby. We were having one of our regular chats and she was venting about several individuals who wanted to be named as the Godfather, she had already chosen a Godmother while still carrying. I was just listening as she let yet another rough statement escape her lips, she stated bluntly, "My child doesn't have a Godfather because I don't know anyone qualified to be her Godfather!" It was so arrogant that it was actually funny. I found it a little offensive, being as though, you know my Godchild; you've been around he and I enough to draw some conclusion about what type of Godparent I am, and quite honestly, you were talking about me too. Although I wasn't one of the contestants in her 'GodParenting Pageant," I had no interest in taking on more godchildren.

The comment was a little bold and braising, to say the least. But again, you cannot be mad at people for how they see you.

When picking your friends and developing your friendships make certain that you have the proper amount of respect involved in the pot, or it will spoil your meal.

When I started thinking about respect as a whole, I realize that I still have an uphill battle when it comes to demanding respect from people. Some damage has been done in the way of friends, of the family and some folks from our community as a whole. This is the result of a lot of that open disrespectful behavior that was distributed by my family as well as non-family members over the years. There was an incident a few years ago at a surprise birthday party for an older woman that I adored. We were standing in the kitchen area, there was six or seven people including myself and we were just chatting and enjoying ourselves when a woman who has been a friend to our family for years entered the kitchen. She took the time to address each individual separately by saying hello and using their name, with me being the last one. When she got to me she

stopped and gave me a look and said, "Oh, I guess you just

wanted to have your hair lookin' wild, huh!" (my hair was

in a curly fro, reminiscent of the singer Maxwell, and it was

in no way, shape or form looking wild.) I was caught a

little off guard by this but not completely shocked, you see

this person has been hanging around my cousins for years

and what has happened is she has learned the bad behavior

and found herself a comfort level within it. The only

problem is she must not have been paying attention to the

parts when I snap out and let them have it, she only tuned

in to the, 'Oh, anybody can say what they want to him!' –

Big Mistake! One of my older male cousins that never

indulged in the bad behavior responded before I could, he

said, "I don't know why you are so preoccupied with his

hair, you don't have any." And all was quiet, she didn't

have a response of any sort, and that is because she was

caught off guard. She didn't even have a response prepared

for me, because in her mind, I was going to take the insult

and that was it. Another female who happened to be one of

the people in the kitchen and seen the whole thing unfold said to me, "I am so proud of you, I thought for sure you were going to turn the party out, and the birthday girl hasn't even arrived yet. You know how you get down." Now how sad is that when you have two people on two different sides of the fence – the fool who thought the bad behavior was cute and wanted to give it a try and the person that has seen the situation over and over for years and realized that the bad behavior is greeted with bad outcomes. Trust me when I tell you our friends and associates are watching how we treat each other as members of a family unit. Later on that evening, a cousin that has indulged in the public disrespect countless number of times and frequently hangs out with the woman spoke about the incident, she said, "I heard what she said and I can't believe she said that to you, who does she think she is!" I refused at that point to give the situation anymore oxygen, so I just said, "You'll have that."

The truth is, she was taught this, by this very person and she never even realized that she had set the stage for this and other incidents herself. It had been years in the making, and the pupil just finally took the initiative and acted as ugly to her teacher's cousin as she has in the past. The question is, should you really be upset with a person for doing exactly what you taught them to do? I've found it to be a very interesting concept.

TEN

<u>Smoke & Mirrors</u>

My home life was very interesting as I reached my twenties, it was a bunch of overactive gripes and ridiculous rules. Everything from what time I came in and went as far as how late my telephone rang during the night, it was ridiculous. One of the biggest character attacks was that I literally was not allowed a male guest in the house, I found this offensive because there was nothing that should have ever been said to me in this area. I was and still happen to be one of the few males that have not had sex under my Grandmother's roof. There was always a constant flow of women escorted through the quarters with my Grandmother's blessings. They ranged from my older cousins moving in for a period and dragging a woman with them, to my Uncle being thrown out by his wife and bringing his adulteress affairs to our house. So when it came to me, why was it that I couldn't have a person come

by and indulge in a conversation in the livingroom? I

found it very demeaning and I spoke up about it on several

occasions. I made sure that I let my Grandmother know, I

was not a teenager but I was grown adult, paying rent

monthly. And more importantly, I would never lay up with

anyone in the midst of a house that has an over-abundance

of keyholders and house guests walking around at all times,

that is just tacky. She really had no rebuttal, she would

basically blow me off whenever the subject arose.

There were times when my Grandmother just went

overboard, such as the time when I decided I'd had enough

of the bogus rules and a guy I was dating came to the house

to pick me up. She knew who he was and he would always

wait in the car for me, this particular day I wasn't feeling

all of her foolishness and I pressed her hand and told him to

come in, because I wasn't quite ready. I was finishing

sewing something and packing my bag. After I fussed

awhile he followed me in the house and up the steps to my

room, I saw the look on her face and just ignored her. It

was about 4:30 p.m. and she was sitting in the livingroom

with my Uncle. As I took care of the things that I had to

and enjoyed the conversation of my friend I kept hearing

this slight bumping at my door, I thought for a minute and

then said to myself, 'Nah, that couldn't be it!' I few

minutes later I stood up and walked across my room and

yanked my door open and in stumbled Miss Thelma,

foolish and in the flesh. I have never been so embarrassed,

I started yelling, "Who does that, who would be at a door

eavesdropping on a conversation that wasn't even

interesting. I hope you learned how to put in a zipper,

cause that's what I was showing him!" She yelled, "I don't

give a fuck what you say, you just keep this damn door

open." I yelled back, "Get a life!" and slammed to door

closed. My friend told me not to worry about it, he had

come to know how sideways my Gram could be. He was a

person who had a job in street pharmaceuticals if you will,

and she knew that. She had a really bad habit of waiting

until he would be out front blowing his horn for me to

come out and she would run up asking me for money and

when I would refuse, he would give it to her. I would get so pissed off at these antics, but he would just say, "Let her have it!" I wanted to let her have it, alright!

When I was younger I wasn't allowed to breathe where my Gram was concerned, I wasn't allowed to spend nights out and nobody was allowed to stay over. She explained to me when I reached my late teens; she said very curt and clear, "I knew what was going on with you, and little boys are nasty – nobody was going to be experimenting with you!" I understood what she meant and she did what she thought was best in the situation, and I guess I'd have to say that it was effective for the most part. The only problem with her tactics was she was targeting the wrong audience. The folks that she should've been watching were right inside with us on a lot of occasions, these folks that I refer to as 'Play Cousins.' They come from everywhere, it can be the cousin of a cousin, from their other side, or the grandchild or child of a friend, or someone that's been around the family possibly longer than you, etc. I told my Grandmother years later when I got in my thirties, "Despite all your efforts, Sweetheart, you brought all the ants to the picnic! It was an uphill battle keeping my virtue intact. I had plenty of offers, I wasn't ready for all of that." For these reasons I never liked wrestling, uh no – open forum for grinding and such – no thanks! You name it, I've heard it, "Can you help me take this necklace off" – and the next thing you know you are locked in the bathroom with a naked fool. Then there was the time period when my bedroom was in the basement of our house, straight foolishness, the clowns that ventured down those steps, please! And the ridiculous offers they'd make – "Yeah, I can make you into the woman you wanna be!" (where'd you get that from – uh, no thanks.) "Oh yeah, if you let me, I can make you walk funny!" (wow, uh, I'll pass.) "You like Popsicles!" (got some upstairs, but thanks anyway.) I never found this mess amusing or acceptable, and that way of talking always made me feel that they thought I was cheap and tawdry, and I was definitely not. My responses were always the same, "You do know that my Mother will hunt you down and my Grandmother will shoot you!" That worked until I was old enough to really let these types know what I really thought of them. I am very protective of my sons now, I don't trust anyone, and they definitely don't do overnight stays.

I felt like someone was in my corner with these situations until I reached a certain age then things shifted and it was more of a 'Guilty til proven Innocent Vibe' going on. My Grandmother was a terrible eavesdropper and an even worse rambler and snoop, she would go through my room and go through my things, but she always blabbed about what she thought she found or discovered. As you can tell from this book, I am not a secretive or a sneaky type of person, so really Miss Thelma, you were finding nothing, because nothing was hidden. There was this particular situation where one of the play cousins had visited over the Thanksgiving holiday and started sending letters to our house, the letters were a little less than innocent, they talked about how I had grown and what wishes he was harboring. There were three letters in total and they had sat in a pile of junk mail for several months and I went through that mess one day and threw them in the garbage in my room and thought no more of it; it was midway through the week and our garbage pickup is Mondays, so I empty my bedroom trash on Sunday; when I came home on that Friday I was blindsided by my Grandmother screaming and yelling, "Now I'm not gonna have this," she was waving the letters in the air. I went from 0 to 10 in about a second, and yelled at her, "Tell me what it is that you're not having lady! Tell me what I did, go ahead, let's get it on, tell me what you're not gonna have, so I can tell you what you're gonna get!" She just looked at me and said, "This shit ain't cute!" I said, "I agree, so now what? You are always snooping and sneaking around and reading must not be one of your strong points or you would've seen that every letter makes reference to no return letters being sent and him wanting them! Leave me alone and go away!" She has never apologized for that, and I didn't deserve that. But I guess that tells a lot of what she thinks my character is, she should know better. But that's her issue, not mine.

When I was 18 there was a situation that took place where my youngest Godsister and I were outside of their house and one of our 'play cousins' approached me in a most inappropriate fashion. He is actually older than she is and she is 10 years older than I am. I could tell that she was a shocked as I was with the boldness of his moves right in her presence. He made statements about he and I needed to hang out and he would make sure that I was taken care of and definitely feeling good, and he would make sure of it cause he knew what I needed, etc. I was kind of waiting for her to check him, but that didn't happen; what happened was she left me outside with him and went in the house. So as he continued giving his pitch for the unthinkable, I was certain that my Godsister would be coming back with one of my Godparents, but she never returned. After I graciously declined his offer and just basically told him that I couldn't do it, because we are cousins and I understand that we are not blood related, but for my whole life I have identified with him as being my cousin and I just couldn't see myself doing that. He was cool and told me to think

about it. I thought about it and YUCK, sorry not a fan!
When I came in the house, I asked, "Why did you leave me
like that?" She said, "I wanted to see what you were going
to do. I couldn't believe him, I was so uncomfortable."
And I responded, "Really, but you left me out there with
him. That's messy!" Sometimes I swear these people
seem to act like they don't know me at all.

The other situation at my house that became a big deal
was 'High Heeled Sneakers' as my Grandmother called it.
This subject actually was a large part of why I did this
book, and has caused me a lot of grief and confusion.
When I was 19, I was attending the Clarissa School of
Fashion Design and I was introduced to a drag queen that
was the current reigning Miss Gay Pittsburgh and he was
interested in having me to do some sewing for him. I'm
not a judgmental person at all so I was game to do it, it was
a job and I definitely could use the cash. I did a gown for a
show for him and then that led to several other projects, he
got me into the bar for my first time to see a show, it was
fabulous and I enjoyed it, and saw all the money that he

made and thought, 'Boy, that's cool.' But I had no interest in trying it. I went on from there and met a guy that was actually going to have a gay wedding and he contracted me to do his wedding gown, it was a fabulous project, we worked on it for months and then I was invited to the wedding which was just as beautiful as any regular heterosexual wedding I'd attended. In the process I had turned 21 and was hanging out with a few new friends and two of them did drag, but only one of them was really serious about it and decided to compete for the Miss Pittsburgh title, I was one his sponsors, and did all his outfits for the pageant, he did a fabulous job and made 1st Runner up. He went on to do numerous shows and I would be right beside him for support. Now this full almost two years my Grandmother would be screaming, "You can do whatever you want, but you better not put on no high heeled sneakers!" She said that over and over and over again. And quite honestly she was wasting her breath, I had never even given drag a second thought. Then in Winter of 1992, I tried my hand at it, and walked away from the stage with hands full of money that said, 'I think you're on to something.' Within the first four months I was being booked for shows on a pretty constant basis and I finally opened up to one cousin and good friend of the family that I had been doing shows, the two of them started coming to every show and kept the secret, but within three months, they blabbed and most of my family was showing up for the shows and we would have a great time. In no time I had made quite a name for myself and the bar where most of the shows were held started to take notice to how much of a following I had and started to make reference to the amount of family support that I had. They knew my Grandmother by name and would always praise her for her family leadership and commend her on the unconditional love given to her Grandson and they would make sure that she was comfortable and taken care of the whole time she was at the bar. She would make politically correct statements when they speak to her during the shows, she would say, "I always told him, he could be anything, just be the best!" It was a pivotal time for me, and it was also strange time; sometimes I think she was a bigger local celebrity than I was. And she ate it up!

But what people didn't know was, it was all smoke and mirrors. While my loving Grandmother was pushing the gay flag up the flagpole, she was blowing smoke up everyone's hind parts. At the time that this was all going on, I was not permitted to get dressed in drag at home nor return home in drag even though she was going to be at the show. It was the most ridiculous thing in the world, you approve but you disapprove, how is that possible at the same time. I believe it was the old, 'What are the neighbors going to say!' The weren't saying any more than they were for all the years that she was rolling up in that same house pissy drunk. I dealt with this foolishness for months and then I eventually moved out, all of her antics with this piled on top of it was just too much to bear, I had to go. The whole situation made me feel a bit inauthentic, it was like I was living the lie alongside my family members who shared this double-face with my Grandmother.

There was nothing wrong with what I was doing, and there still isn't, I haven't hurt anyone, I haven't broken any laws. As a matter of a fact I have accomplished great things with my drag persona, my official stage name is Milan Tre'Zur. I have performed extensively throughout the Pittsburgh and the surrounding areas, many parts of West Virginia, various parts of Ohio including Cleveland, Dayton, Akron, Toledo and Youngstown, and I've also graced stages in Philadelphia, and Washington D.C. I have nine pageant wins under my belt to date, (and yes Miss Gay Pittsburgh is one of them.) two pageants that I created and operate on my own, I have been featured in the Pittsburgh Tribune Review newspaper, over the years I have raised thousands of dollars toward HIV/AIDS research and awareness, and I have also starred in an independent film called 'Out Loud.' I am very proud of my accomplishments and the experiences I have had and the knowledge that I have gathered doing female impersonation. And my ship is still sailing, I can't wait to see what's in store for me next!

161

ELEVEN

Who's Zoomin' Who

Dating within the gay community is a really detailed thing, and most people do not realize or understand how complex this process is. Not only is it complex, it also happens to be very discriminatory, I realized early in my twenties, that the heterosexual community could in no way, shape or form discriminate against us in the magnitude that we discriminate against one another!

Most people believe if you have a feminine male and a masculine male, you pair them together and you come up with a happy life. This is so far from the truth! Surely that couple exists somewhere on the planet, but there are not many, for the most part that is a fairytale. I will attempt to break this down in a way that is understandable without leaving anybody out or offending anyone. The breakdown is sometimes so severe that it sometimes gives me a headache. Here we go…

The reality is, there are many labels that have been created within the gay community. Here are some, but not all…

Queen

Butch Queen

Drag Queen

Fem Queen or Tranny

Cross-Dressers

Trade

DL or Closeted Gay Male(On the down low)

and for bedroom purposes

Top

Bottom

Versatile

Versatile – Top

Versatile – Bottom

There's the community, now let me try to explain…

Queen – A homosexual that is feminine in appearance. (A sissy)

Butch Queen – A homosexual that is masculine in appearance. (A sissy with muscles)

Drag Queen – A homosexual that on occasion dresses in women's garments, generally for stage shows, pageants, contests, etc.

Fem Queen/Tranny – A homosexual that is transitioning, or going through the process of becoming a woman. They generally live and identify as a female. (Generally have real breasts by this time)

Cross-Dresser – Generally identify as straight but enjoy wearing women's garments.

Trade – A person who identifies as heterosexual, but has an appetite for gay sex.

DL/Closeted Gay Male – A homosexual that portrays themselves at all times as a heterosexual. Generally would never attend gay clubs or events.

Okay, now this is where it gets really twisted to follow, but we will give it a shot, follow along with me. This is a breakdown of the dating scenarios, and there are many…

Queen – will partner with Trade, Butch Queens and DL/Closeted Gay Males.

Butch Queen – will partner with everybody; but mostly prefer each other.

Drag Queen – will partner with Trade, Butch Queens and DL/Closeted Gay Males.

Fem Queen/Tranny – will partner with Trade, Butch Queens, DL/Closeted Gay Males and men that identify themselves as heterosexual (sometimes referred to a Tranny Chasers).

Cross-Dresser – dates within the heterosexual community.

Trade – will partner with everybody, but takes no one seriously.

So there you have it, I know it makes heterosexuality look like a snap! Just don't cheat and you're good to go!

When it comes to the dating situation all of the breakdown and stipulations have always bothered me, I find it so unnecessary. And of course there are exceptions to every rule, just as with everything else in life.

Myself personally have only been burned by the breakdown one time, and that was enough. And it occurred when against my better judgment, I decided to carry on a long distance relationship. Much to my surprise it was wonderful. My partner lived 3 ½ hours away, and he was pretty much everything that I required to make me happy and more. We spoke on the phone several times a day (this was before the cell phone days) and although I worked for a reputable long distance company and had access to various discounts, he supplied me with the calling cards to cover the cost of my calls. He too, had a decent paying job, I was always receiving little gifts and trinkets by mail and it was really a day for a spoiled brat when he showed up in Pittsburgh on one of his weekend visits. He took on the travel role because he didn't mind the train ride, where as at the time I wasn't much of a traveler. And one big factor was I owned my own home and he was staying with his parents. This for me was not an option; I would not even consider staying at his parents' home. We went very strong and full speed ahead for about eight months without one bump in the road, nor a sign of any trouble. I was swept away with my long distance love. We had actually set a date for him to move to Pittsburgh; he had put in for a transfer of his position at his job and it was granted; the location was only 10 –15 minutes away from my home. Everything was perfect, until I made my one and only trip to Harrisburg to visit my beau. He took care of everything, I was in a very nice hotel, and he was just as happy as a lark that I was actually there in his city. I introduced him to my cousin's ex-wife, who had driven up with me, she has family members that she was going to spend the weekend with. Once we dropped my cousin off, the fun began, but was short lived. I was excited to finally meet his closest friends that evening at dinner. About twenty minutes or so into it, he excused himself to go use the restroom and while he was away, one of the friends said to me, "Excuse me, but can I ask you a personal question?" I replied, "Sure, of course." He said, "Do you do drag?" I was a little thrown of by the question, but answered, "What made you ask me that?" He said, "Your eyebrows are very thin," I replied, "Yes they are, that's the way they've always been, my brothers' are the same, but to answer your question, yes I do." He said, " I thought so, well did you know that Jeremy doesn't like drag queens?" I didn't have a response, I was just kind of sitting there for a moment when the friend continued to make the public announcement to the other six friends that were in attendance, "Hey guys, James does drag. Did any of you know that?" By this time my beau was returning and I guess he could see in my face that I was not a happy camper. The table suddenly became quiet, like a pink elephant had been set free. Jeremy sat down in his seat and kind of whispered to me, "What's wrong Babe, is everything okay?" I kept my voice down as I gritted through my teeth, "Everything is just perfect." I was not going to snap out and ruin the gathering, and besides I was still trying to wrap my mind around what had just happened. A few seconds later the friend dove in for

seconds, he blurted out, "James just shared with us that he

does drag and I was telling him how much you don't like

drag queens." Blank faces surrounded the table awaiting

my response, all the pale muted faces reminded me of the

opening scene from the Nip/Tuck television series. My

Harrisburg smooth-talker, took hold of my hand and

caressed it as he spoke, "It's not like that at all. I mean, I

don't really like drag shows, and all my friends are aware

of that." I said, "That's really nice, but what does any of

that have to do with me?" More quiet moments went by

and then I said, "Why do I feel as though, all of a sudden, I

am a part of previously planned dialogue. Jeremy, would

you mind telling me what my next lines are..." The denials

swirled around the table at an alarming speed, as the

mannequins turned into character witness puppets for how

good of a person Mr. Jeremy was and how he would never

do anything like that, which completely confirmed for me

that I was being played like a fiddle by these folks. To be

honest, I think I was more hurt by the nerve of them feeling as thought they were a swift enough bunch to pull it off! I think NOT!

Needless to say, once I got back to Pittsburgh I broke the relationship up into a million little pieces. I had over three hours in a car to go back and forth over what had happened, why it happened and what my part was in it. And on this I found no blame to be mine, everything was as strange as it seemed, Jeremy knew everything that there was to know about me. He would demand that I called him no matter what time it was when I had shows and performances to do. He would ask how the show went and want to make sure that I got home okay, etc. And to think that all this time you were dying about it on the inside, who does that?

He didn't just let it go, he did fight for the relationship, but how could I trust him with anything or possibly live in a home with someone who keeps that type of information to themselves for that period of time and then use such a cheap television drama climax to bring it out. It was all a bit too dramatic and underhanded for my liking. And then he had the gall to actually ask me if I would choose him over drag. Who would ever think that drag would be a deciding factor to life with or without a person? He went the whole spectrum with it – the whole if you really loved me you could do that one thing, to which I returned, 'And if you had a lick of sense you would realize that I don't sit around in drag, I do shows and pageants, duh. If you don't like it, don't come to the show, because it surely isn't gonna come to you!'

There is no love involved when a person will ask you to sacrifice a part of what makes you-you. And to give up good, legitimate income, chile please!!!!!

TWELVE

<u>God Is REAL!!!!!</u>

There are a lot of things that I question in this life, one thing that I never feel the need to question is the presence of God in my life. He is there all the time, I don't know how anyone could doubt that, all you have to do is look around you. Yes there are a lot of things that are not to your liking I'm sure of that, we all have our likes and dislikes, but stop for minute and take in all of the unexplained beauty that surrounds us, it just didn't happen by chance. I could go on about this for another twenty chapters but that's for another time.

After the successful adoptions of my children I realized how blessed I have been over the years that I have been on this planet. I leaped some pretty tall personal mountains in both of my adoptions. I literally had issues with my Mother's sister and my first cousin's lesbian lover making bogus reports and accusations to Child and Youth Services to try and stop my adoption of my first child. They claimed that I wasn't feeding my baby and keeping him away from the family. The comedy was the child was clearly fed and the agency preferred that these specific individuals not be anywhere near the child, due to past turmoil between the two of them. Whenever a report is made, no matter what or how ridiculous, that agency has to investigate. I understood the position of the agency but it was very trying to have to sit through that turmoil when I was having multiple home visits per month from several agencies that were handling the adoption process, and my workers knew the reports were bogus, but we had to go through the motions. This foolishness held up the adoption process by six months. But he was successfully adopted, after a two year period, despite their vicious attempts. It was amazing to me how two people who profess to hate each other would get together to try to make sure that I was not successful in doing what I was doing. And neither one had a reason to attack me, or the (at that time) 18 month old child.

My oldest child's official adoption took place on a Saturday, and his mother (my first cousin) gave birth to my youngest child that following Tuesday, and I brought him home the next day, which happened to be the day before Thanksgiving, he was only twelve hours old. We literally never had our files put away, we ended up with all the same workers on our case, which was a good thing, I had good people working with me. I was told that the adoption for the baby would be seamless and should take no more than five months. Well 3 ½ months in, like some horrific déjà vu, the adoption was being contested by the paternal father and my first cousin backing him up (because she couldn't, due to her rights being involuntarily terminated.) The paternal father had wound up in jail and was basically trying to use the baby to get an early release, period. After another two year fight, my youngest child was successfully adopted. It was a very stressful four years of my life and I know without a Higher Power in my corner I could've

never come out on the winning end of that process.
Knowing this is what prompted me to begin my search to
find a church home for me and my boys.

I started off by following my Godmother to her church
back when I only had one child, which consists of a small
neighborhood congregation and most of them are up in age.
I had been attending steadily for quite a few months and it
was comfortable, but it never really moved my spirit,
something was missing that I couldn't quite put my hands
on. Then one Sunday, my oldest child's Godfather decided
to join us for service. There was immediately a fakeness
that entered the space, folks who do not ever stop and talk
to me all had a few words to say and tried to introduce
themselves to him. Only problem with that is most them
had never introduced themselves formally to me. I just
kept it moving and didn't say a word until getting ready to
leave the church that afternoon and the pastor stopped
Derrick, the baby and I at the door and said, "I'd like to
thank you fellows for fellowshipping with us, and
remember whatever you are doing wrong the Lord can

deliver you from it." Well that was it, I'd had it, and Derrick saw my eyebrow raise and whispered, "Please Shaft, please don't." The pastor went on, "I was at a card game when the Lord called me and delivered me." At that point I couldn't take anymore, I said, "Derrick I'm sorry but I haven't asked this man one thing about cards and don't really want to hear anymore about it." The pastor just looked at us as I gave him my back and took my baby and walked out of the church. I did not return to the church and after a few weeks got a phone call from my Godmother asking why I hadn't come and I explained to her what happened, she said she had already heard, but she wanted it from my mouth. I had told my Grandmother what happened and she told another cousin that goes to the church how she felt about it and that cousin had also noticed that I hadn't been to church and told my Godmother of the conversation that my Gram and her had. My Godmother told me that she fully intended to talk with her pastor and let him know that I was offended, though she tried to convince me that he didn't mean anything by it, I didn't buy into that at all and told her don't worry about it because I had no intentions on giving that pastor or that church anymore of my sinful, pink money ever again, and maybe one day I would attend a service but not right now. There was no way to explain that situation, I was being unfairly judged and that pastor was out of order and he was 500% wrong in his perception of Derrick and I. Derrick is my child's Godfather and that is it, we have no type of romantic dealings with each other and never have. I have personally been celibate since 2002 and I do not date at all. So the Lord didn't send him our way with that bogus message, the Lord doesn't make those kinds of mistakes. I didn't return to the church for two years. Then my Godmother told me of their new pastor, a woman of God and so anointed. I dropped my guard and said, "I'll give her a chance." I began attending services steadily again, I still wasn't getting exactly what I was looking for, but it was pleasant. I now had two children and was dealing with a bit of stress from the second adoption process. This particular Sunday I went down to the altar for prayer, and my stomach was turned with disgust when this woman laid

hands on me and started into a rant about the Lord

delivering me from the confusion that I have that's

plaguing my life, and letting me walk and be who God

wants me to be, and so on and so on. I opened my eyes as

soon as she went into her rant, because that is what it was,

it wasn't a prayer for me it was a self-indulgent rant and I

was mortified and I left that day and that was it for me. Of

course my Godmother had some excuse, I told my

Godmother, nothing would get me back to that church.

A few weeks later I was invited to another church for

the ordination of one of my cousins, from the moment I

stepped in that church there was something in me stirring. I

had never heard of the church and knew none of the

congregation. It was run by a female pastor and her

husband, I'd never seen that dynamic before, but it was

refreshing and cool. It showed what they preached; God

will use anyone to serve him and titles really don't matter.

There was a spirit moving through that church on that day

that was undeniable, by the time they had finished the

service I had went down center to join and become a part of the congregation. I went all in I started attending and learning tons of things about the church and how it runs, it really can dominate a lot of your time. Sunday service, personal counsel with the pastor on Tuesday, Friday evening service, Wednesday Bible Study and there is usually something going on after church on Sunday. But I was there everytime the doors opened, I loved the fact that we had four different pastors and all of their styles were very different, so you could get the standpoint of each one. And no one was judging you and trying to change you. Everything was going well until one Sunday that was my cousin's week to preach, before she even got started there was a point that she was claiming that the spirit was leading her to pray for this teenage girl. The girl was a member of our church and was clearly a lesbian, my cousin began into a rant about how the girl was dressed and how girls should be with boys and not other girls and she just went on and on until I couldn't take another word of it, so I got up and left. The next day I was contacted by my pastor and told that I needed to come in for a meeting with her to discuss

what had gone one. I showed up for the meeting, and right

before we got started, my cousin, the Associate Pastor

showed up. I immediately caught on that this was an

ambush, and I felt violated and attacked – two things that

have never worked well for me. The Pastor started by

saying, "I've been waiting to discuss this subject with you,

and you can't do that," I said, "Do what?" She sat up in her

chair and said, "Everytime the sermon isn't to your liking

you can't get up and leave. You have to stay and listen to,

thus sayeth the Lord." I said, "And who says that, who said

that I can't get up and leave anywhere, for any reason that I

choose. And I have never read in the Bible anywhere about

sitting somewhere uncomfortable, while someone spews

venom all over the sanctuary, and I won't do that. It didn't

matter to me who is preaching, I will always leave when

what is being done or said is not sit well in my spirit. And I

will not answer for that. What was being done in that

pulpit in my eyes was out of order and I was not going to

have that child believe that I was in agreement with the

treatment that she received and I would have never accepted it." She said, "Well, why do you think that something was out of order?" I replied, "There was no reason for her to be put out there like that in front of the whole church, and if she was going to be ridiculed that way, why wasn't every person that was dealing with the affliction called onto the carpet." My cousin preceded to gather her things to leave and said, "Oh I thought we were have a Bible Study." I said, "Bible Study is on Wednesday not Monday and how often do you make it anyway." She didn't respond she just gathered her daughter and her things and left. She knew that my mouth was getting ready to make it's way around the room. After she was gone my pastor went into some business about homosexuality and it being wrong and she kept saying, "You gave your life to the Lord and you don't have to do that anymore." I explained to her that just because I gave myself to the Lord didn't stop me from being gay." Well that created the battle, she swore I had been delivered from my homosexuality. I assured her that she hadn't delivered me from a thing because I was looking to be delivered, I had

no issue with my sexuality and never have. I assured her

that, when in comes to men, I liked them and wasn't

interested in changing that. Then I hit her with the question

that always tends to stump the gospel panel, "Is the

supposed sin that I am attracted to men or does the sin

occur when I partake in homosexual activity with a man." I

lost a lot of the trust that I had previously for my pastor.

The fact that she had sat and waited for what she deemed as

the best time to talk to me about the homosexuality piece I

thought was petty. And it just didn't sit right with me. It

just seemed a little underhanded and the ambush really

turned me off. Now that's not to take anything away from

how I felt about her as a person, I was absolutely crazy

about her up until the day a she passed away in 2012, and I

miss her like crazy. I just feel as though church is like an

exclusive group that gays will never fit into completely, it

doesn't matter how much good you do, or stand for, there

will always be a pink elephant in the room with your name

on it. So what I gather is, this is one of those times when

you cannot allow anyone to deter you from your happiness, you need to find a church that you can stomach, where the shade throwing distracts you the least, and when you feel up to it, go and worship – worship until your soul can't hardly stand it! God is real and he deserves your praise, and he welcomes it – no matter who you are. He is waiting to hear from you!

THIRTEEN

<u>Death Of A Donor</u>

I have just been given information on a man that I would refer to, with all due respect as a sperm donor. His name is Robert Garner, and he is my paternal Father. I was just told by one of my family members on Thursday, October 3, 2013 in the early afternoon that my donor had passed away about a month ago. He was really shocked that I had no clue.

Though I have nothing against him, I don't have any feelings for him either. I didn't know him, if I had walked up to him face to face three months ago I wouldn't have known who I was speaking to. The last time I seen my donor was when I was twelve years old and he was dropping off paperwork about my medical coverage to my Grandmother's house. He didn't even try to see me he rang the bell, placed the papers in the doorway and I caught a glimpse of him from the back as he walked away down our driveway. I never saw his face. The mental picture I have of my paternal Father is of him walking down the driveway and not looking back, which is irony, because that's what he did in my life. For reasons that had nothing to do with me personally, he turned his back and walked away without ever turning around.

An agreement was formed by two adults about a baby boy, it was simple, whenever I need funding for this child, I will contact you and you will provide the funding needed. Everything went well until my donor didn't hold up to his side of the agreement on the child's tenth year when he was asked to provide funding of $500.00 for him to attend a Saturday computer class. And meanwhile, he literally had not seen this child in over eight years. Once it was made very clear that there was no interest in relations between the two adults, interest in the child fell to the wayside as well, but he had always kept up his part of the agreement, until now. And at that point, my Mother kept her promise as stated in the previous agreement and sued him for child

support.

So, at the age of 10, I had the one and only experience

that I would ever have with my paternal Father, as he stood

in a courtroom hearing and denied paternity. I was not in

the courtroom that day, but in the weeks to come I would

be taken out of school and driven to a site to have blood

work taken to test my DNA. This situation to date is the

most humiliating thing that I have ever had to undergo.

The test came back absolutely positive for a paternity

match and my donor was ordered to now pay $200.00

every month for the full extent of my adolesence. I have

never figured out what point he was trying to make with

that action, because in the end, he really harmed himself.

Up to that point he wasn't spending anywhere near the now

$2400.00 per year and I had to be added on to his

insurance, which was an additional cost.

I have to laugh at the situation because of the fact that it

is so demeaning, at least I didn't have to stomach it being

on television. My situation happened in 1982, thank God,

Jerry Springer and Maury Povich didn't have the idea to do this on the air until 1991. Thank goodness.

Quite a few years back when I was an employee for the phone company I met a young woman and found out after we worked there for about four years that we were second cousins. She actually knew on the third year, but didn't have the heart to say anything and then one day she said she couldn't bite her tongue anymore and couldn't let me walk around not knowing who my family was. At that point Aretha invited me to her house for the Christmas holiday. After much thought I decided to show up, and I really had a nice time. I met cousins and aunts, but my donor wasn't there and neither were my half siblings. Aretha gave me a little background, but I always knew that I had an older sister and a younger sister. What I didn't know is that my older sister actually knew everything that there was to know about me and wanted nothing to do with me, because she felt as though having a gay brother was an embarrassment. Just recently I figured out why that comment doesn't really bother me, there is no face to put with the situation, so how personal could I take it really. For a grown woman to go out of the way to gather information on a half sibling and then sift through the information and decide what works for her purpose and what doesn't seems a little sad and that's not the kind of relationship that I am interested in building with anyone.

The fact is I am not upset with my donor or any of his children, they are actually strangers to me and don't owe me a thing. The weird thing is they know who I am and what I look like, we live in the same area of town, I have probably seen these people and didn't even realize they were my family. I look at it this way, the burden is there's because when they see me they are forced to live in that realm of denial and I don't have to suffer any of the stress related with that false state of being, because I'm not living any lies. And just a side note, he was 98.9% proof positive; my parent, just like he was to them and none of us can change that. Genetics bust secrets and lies open everytime.

FOURTEEN

The Journey Continues

For years I have cringed at stories of individuals being thrown away and disowned by their families for being **DIFFERENT**. But in the last few years I have found myself wrestling with the questions – Would it have been easier for me if my family had just turned their back on me? What have I gained by trying to keep my family ties with these individuals that clearly do not care about me the way they should?

This has been a learning experience for me, and possibly the hardest thing that I have ever decided to do. Reliving and rehashing old feelings and painful memories was no trip through the park, the truth is never easy.

When the truth shows up you can guarantee, someone is going to get hurt, someone is going to get upset, and someone is going to disagree but what is more important is, someone is going to receive clarity, someone is going to be inspired, someone is going to make better choices and someone is going live another day.

While writing this book I have laughed, I have cried, I have paced the floor in anger and in confusion, but best of all I have learned.

I've learned that my journey is far from over, everytime I am blessed to open my eyes, I truly have one more time to get it right. I've learned that everything that happened was the set up for something great that has happened or will happen. I've learned that it doesn't matter why or how folks did the things that they did, what matters is, I understand that, ultimately, whatever they did, was what they wanted! And now the baggage is not mine to carry. I've learned that nothing is an accident; I am who I am today because I am the best one for the job. This assignment couldn't be carried out by anyone else but **A Boy Like Me**!

Also Available from James

Colwell

Loving Topaz

Losing Topaz

Learning Topaz

Between Pews

www.JCNovels.com

CPSIA information can be obtained
at www.ICGtesting.com
Printed in the USA
LVOW13s1030200217
524800LV00015B/421/P